Christian Plowman is a decorated ex-police officer with 16 years investigative experience, mainly in the covert arena. A specialist in undercover operations and recruitment and management of informants, he spent years working in a variety of roles for Scotland Yard. Since leaving the police, Christian has worked in the private sector. He currently works overseas as a national security manager for a fashion company.

CROSSING THE LINE
LOSING YOUR MIND AS AN UNDERCOVER COP

CHRISTIAN PLOWMAN

MAINSTREAM PUBLISHING

EDINBURGH AND LONDON

First published in Great Britain in 2013 by

MAINSTREAM PUBLISHING COMPANY

(EDINBURGH) LTD

7 Albany Street

Edinburgh EH1 3UG

ISBN 9781780576275

This book is a work of non-fiction based on the life, experiences and
recollections of the author. In some cases names of people, places, dates,
sequences or the detail of events have been changed to protect the privacy of
others. The author has stated to the publishers that, except in such respects, not
affecting the substantial accuracy of the work, the contents of this book are true

A catalogue record for this book is available
from the British Library

Printed in Great Britain by
CPI Group (UK) Ltd, Croydon, CR0 4YY

1 3 5 7 9 10 8 6 4 2

This book is dedicated to Max and Vinnie – I hope you understand now – and to Albie and Amelia (spy kids!), as well as DGB

CONTENTS

AUTHOR'S NOTE

ALL OF THE EVENTS IN THE BOOK ACTUALLY HAPPENED.
I have changed the names and characteristics of most people
in the book. I have also changed some of the locations and
lots of the police methodology, and I have been careful not
to divulge any sensitive information.

It's important to let you know a couple of things before
we go on. I don't want to use loads of police terms and
acronyms. But you need to know a few, because they are
unavoidable.

So let me introduce you to the term 'undercover' first.
'Undercover', 'UC' or 'UCO' (undercover officer) means
someone who is operating with a different identity in order
to gather evidence against a criminal or criminals, essentially.
When I was working as a plain-clothes officer, we would
often get referred to as 'undercovers' by local oiks or the
media. UCOs don't have radios, batons or warrant cards.
They are someone else for the time they are undercover.
It's not 'plain clothes'. They don't have blue lights and
nee-naws in their cars. They are utterly secretive and live
in another world, with different names, different addresses
and different ways of life. Cool, eh?

Now here's another: 'test purchase officer'. A test purchase officer (TP or TPO) is another type of undercover officer. They will go out and buy small amounts of street drugs (like crack, heroin or cocaine) to gather evidence against drug dealers. Also they can present themselves as prostitutes or drunken potential robbery victims. It's seen as a lower level of undercover work and is certainly less glamorous than being a UCO. Often, TPOs are scorned and looked down on by UCOs. Not many UCOs have also been TPOs, although lots of TPOs aspire to be UCOs. Are you with me so far? TPOs have no radios or warrant cards or anything. A TPO will often be on the streets for only half an hour or so before they've made a purchase of drugs, whereas some UC officers live and breathe their other life, sometimes for years at a time.

SO10, SCD10, Covert Ops, whatever you want to call it, is seen as the elite of the Met. It is a small department, responsible for, amongst other things, training test purchase officers, overseeing and advising on undercover operations, recruiting, training and managing undercover officers in London, nationwide and internationally, and running the secretive Undercover Unit.

At its heart is a tiny office staffed by several detective sergeants who are also known as 'cover officers'. It is their responsibility to oversee and advise on undercover jobs, select suitable UC officers for those jobs and monitor and assess their performance and welfare.

They also train test purchase officers and run the Met test purchase course. Although the recruitment and training system and the names of the courses have recently changed, the principles remain the same.

It's a well-worn joke that the SO10 office is not big enough for the egos of the staff. They are often embarrassingly arrogant and impolite to outsiders (i.e. those who are not UCs), including senior officers and experienced TP officers. Even as a fully fledged UC officer, with seven years of doing TP work under my belt, I was often ignored and talked down to – usually by officers who were supposed to be responsible for my well-being. The vast majority of the SO10 staff are big, shaven-headed white blokes in their 40s. They operate in a very intimidating and macho atmosphere, where japes, jibes and un-PC comments abound. There is little politeness from some officers, and it's a culture that has been in existence since the inception of the Undercover Unit. There have been innumerable attempts to change it, but all to no avail. They see themselves as the elite, and quite rightly. Some of them have been in situations that you would not be able to imagine, using only their wits and charm to wheedle out of them.

The favoured dress is Stone Island and Prada Sport, with a smattering of North Face, or, if you're lucky, maybe a bit of Ralph Lauren or Armani. Chunky bracelets and Rolexes are the order of the day, along with a standard-issue south-east London accent; lots of chat about 'slaughters' (lockups) and 'drums' (houses) and 'snouts' (informants) is common. Sometimes it is rather like being in a spoof episode of *The Sweeney*. All the DSs in this office are experienced UC officers, although some haven't worked for years. They regale one another with tales of derring-do, usually trying to outdo one another.

The office runs a fleet of covert cars and, natch, they have to be top of the range. The DSs get the pick of the bunch, all Range Rovers, 7 Series BMWs and Audis. They operate with a lot of autonomy and have a huge amount of influence in the specialist operations arena. They run training courses all over the world and are often jetting off abroad to exotic climes. I always felt that any sign of non-compliance with their ideals, of not fitting in with their world or of weakness, like 'stress' or suchlike, would not be tolerated. Kiss goodbye to a career in covert ops if you displayed a bit of sensitivity!

This is the story of my fateful journey into the maelstrom.

PROLOGUE

SCUTTLING ALONG THE STREET, CHATTING WITH ALAN, I felt the two tenners getting warm in my filthy hand. With every step, I was aware of the odour of dirt and urine from my mud-caked jeans. My battered Reebok Classics scuffed the ground, the frayed laces trailing on the pavement.

We walked with purpose, keen to get our next fix. Alan told me that we might have to wait a while in the flat we were going to. I sniffed and lit up a cigarette as we walked. Alan shouted a greeting to a girl meandering along in the opposite direction. Emaciated, with vacant, red-rimmed eyes, she was most likely a crack whore.

'You going to D's?' she squeaked.

'Yeah,' said Alan. 'Is anything about?'

'In a minute, I reckon,' she said, hawking up a great glob of phlegm and depositing it on the pavement. She looked at me and mumbled a greeting, taking in my lank hair, tired eyes, reddened nose and scabbed lips and fingers, the nails of which were encrusted with grime.

'Got a fag?' she asked.

'Course,' I said, pulling out a battered pack of Bensons.

She took one and, sparking it with a lighter from the pocket of her cropped leather jacket, simply wandered off, without a word of thanks. Alan puffed and panted as we walked on quickly. We didn't want to miss the drop.

'What you getting, Al?' I asked.

'One of each,' said Alan.

'Me too,' I said.

We turned into a side road and found ourselves in front of a six-storey block of flats, the sort where the front doors are arranged along an open passageway visible from the street.

'Don't tell me,' I said. 'Top floor?'

'Yes, son.' He smiled.

With no small effort, we trudged up the dank, dark stairwells to the top floor. We walked along the passageway. Anyone could have guessed our destination from our appearance; we were heading for number 36, the flat with the peeling paint, boarded windows and tell-tale damage on the door from police battering-rams.

The queasiness I always felt in these situations started to return – fear of the unknown, of what was waiting for me behind this door.

What we did know was that the guy who ran this place was known to give people a slap if he didn't like them. Luckily, Alan had been here a couple of times before, so, in theory, we shouldn't have any problems getting served up.

Alan knocked firmly. In a moment, we heard the sound of locks being drawn open behind the door. A solidly built black lad opened it. He simply nodded and we made our way through to the front room.

To say what greeted us was a tableau of human desperation

would be an understatement. It was a scene few people, save for those who were part of the seedy hard drugs underclass, would ever understand. Fellow junkies, about 15 in all, sat and stood around. We were all waiting for 'D' to arrive with his stash.

I gingerly sat on the bare, dirty floor. There was no furniture. The room was dark, because of the council grilles attached to the windows. The sole sources of illumination were a scintilla of daylight squeezing through a gap in the metal and the occasional flare of a lighter when someone lit a cigarette or crack pipe.

We all spoke amongst ourselves, with only one topic of conversation: drugs. Smack or crack, brown or white, one and one, one of each? It was all anyone cared about. We spoke endlessly about the quality, the price, smoking it, digging it, the difference in gear between here and the West End. Over the course of about two hours, we were joined by an increasingly desperate band of ne'er-do-wells, society's flotsam and jetsam.

The black guy at the door was harassed at regular intervals.

'Where's D?'

'How long?'

'When's he gonna be here?'

His response was always the same: 'Soon.'

Some of the more connected people were making calls to D, asking him for his whereabouts, then reassuring the assembled punters with a cheery: 'Five minutes. Be here in five.'

D, it appeared, was a good marketing man, understanding the rule of supply and demand, knowing that if he maximised his customer base by keeping them waiting, they would buy more.

Five minutes after five minutes passed. Eventually, a whisper spread through the throng.

'He's here, he's here.'

Our lives would soon be complete. Our high was nigh. We heard the door being unlocked and opened. A large, thickset black lad entered, probably only about 19 years old, wearing the customary street uniform of New Era baseball cap, Nike tracksuit and Air Force Ones. The group was unsettled and everyone scrambled up from their sitting positions. Despite the desperation, there was evidently an informal queuing system, as preference was given to those who had been there the longest, myself and Alan included. We found ourselves in front of D fairly quickly and I proffered my two sweaty ten-pound notes.

'One of each, bruv,' I said.

D took my cash and opened his left hand to reveal about 40 small wraps, each the size of a small pea, some wrapped in blue plastic and some in clear to differentiate between heroin and crack.

'Make them big ones, bruv,' I pleaded to D as he selected one of each colour wrap and handed them to me. I gleefully stuffed them into my pocket and watched Alan conduct a similar transaction. Just as Al had been given his gear, a loud banging was heard on the door and the door guy hurriedly let the excited caller in. The visitor, a shorthaired woman with an obvious drug problem, gulped in a huge lungful of air, her pasty, gaunt face covered in sweat, and almost deliriously she blurted, 'Police! The Old Bill are here!'

The words were still hanging in the air when the door imploded with an enormous crash.

In milliseconds, hordes of riot cops burst in, screaming

and shouting, ordering everyone to show their hands. Their heavy-duty uniforms made them seem massive. Some people resisted and were thrown to the floor. Amid the noise and chaos, I squeezed myself into a corner, hands raised. Near shitting myself, I looked around nervously. A massive cop, helmet on and visor down, his features masked by his flameproof balaclava, grabbed my left arm and twisted it. 'On the fucking floor!' he shouted, forcing me onto my face.

'Fuck,' I thought. His knee pressed into my shoulder as he knelt on top of me, pinning both my arms behind me and handcuffing me. My cheek was pushed hard into the floor. At once, I was handcuffed. I could feel the grit and dirt from the filthy floorboards on my skin.

Struggling for breath and acutely aware of my vulnerability, I tried to move a bit, but the big cop sat on me harder, shouting, 'Stop resisting!'

He twisted the handcuffs, causing the nerves in my arms to spasm.

I screamed, 'Ow! For fuck's sake! Alan, what the fuck are they doing?'

I heard Alan shout back, 'Don't worry, son, don't worry.'

This was swiftly followed by a command from one of Alan's captors: 'Shut the fuck up.'

Big Cop then rifled through my pockets and found my aging Nokia 3310, which he dropped to the floor, causing the battery to fall out. Then, of course, he hit pay dirt, finding my little ten-pound wraps of heroin and crack in my pocket. Even though I couldn't see his face, I could sense his glee.

'You're nicked, mate. Possession of Class A.'

He twisted my cuffs even tighter, causing me to grimace in pain again as my cheek scraped deeper into the floor. I started hurting all over. This was not going to plan at all. My day was going to be ruined.

'The fucking prick,' I thought.

'Wasn't he at the briefing? Doesn't he know I'm one of his fucking colleagues?'

1
GROWING UP

SPORTING GREY SHORTS, GREY SOCKS AND A SMARTLY
ironed green jumper emblazoned with Cub Scout badges, I
adjusted my woggle and scarf before leaving the church hall.
Intending to wander through the back streets homewards, I
greedily shoved bubblegum into my mouth, the spoils of two
ten-pence pieces I had found under my mum's bed.

I meandered into the High Road, taking in the hordes
of police, some wearing unusual helmets with visors,
running along the street in groups. I only fleetingly noticed
the clunk of missiles landing at their feet and the gaggle
of mainly black lads shouting abuse at the cops.

Thinking little of it, as one does when one is eight years
old, I merrily skipped home, squeezing through a roadblock
of armoured police carriers, heading towards Broad Lane
before turning right along West Green Road.

As I lazily strolled along, I could hear the clunk and
smash of things hitting the ground behind me. 'Pigs,' I
thought to myself, not really knowing what it meant. The
only real interactions I had had with the police were when
I'd got robbed aged five and when my mate Michael and
I used to throw conkers at policemen on CND marches in

central London, a common jaunt in those days, supervised by Michael's über-hippy, ultra-left-wing mother. I just thought it was a bit of a jolly jape, really.

This was Tottenham. This was my home. I saw the riots later on the news. It was one of those times in my childhood when we could afford a TV, albeit a black-and-white one.

Sparked by the death of an African Caribbean woman called Cynthia Jarrett, whose heart failed during a police search of her home on the Broadwater Farm estate, the riots became notorious in Britain because of a second loss of life that day. Constable Keith Blakelock was stabbed to death after being set upon by a gang of about 50 marauding youths when he slipped while beating a retreat from the violent mob. He became the first police officer to be murdered in a riot on the streets of Britain since 1833.

Being such a young chap, I barely registered that this was all happening on my doorstep. Broadwater Farm was unknown to me, despite the fact that a few of my primary school chums lived there. Danny and Tyrone, however, still met up with me at Wood Green shopping centre on Saturdays to coo lovingly over the Gabicci jumpers, Pierre Cardin jackets, Sergio Tacchini tracksuits and Diadora trainers in the shops there. They didn't appear to be bothered by the riot, so it didn't affect me.

Three years later, I was wandering along the same stretch of West Green Road proudly wearing my new uniform, complete with pressed slacks, tie and purple-and-black striped blazer. It was clear to the local youngsters that I did not go to school round here. Three slightly older lads walked brazenly up to me and the plump ringleader slapped me round the face.

'You fucking posh cunt,' he said.

More shocked by the slap than the language, I stammered, 'W-w-what?'

'What gay school do you fucking go to?' he asked, as his mates jeered.

'I dunno,' I said nervously, trying to walk round him.

'Fuck you, gay boy,' he spat angrily, before shoving me into a hedge and running off laughing. Red-faced and bursting with tears, I was worried that maybe I had ripped the blazer – only available in Harrods, you know – that my mum had worked her arse off to buy.

It was a situation she was getting used to – working hard to buy essentials for my sister and me. My parents split up when I was 13. My dad, who went on to become a renowned sculptor, left home and I've only seen him three or four times since then. Mum had been 16 when she had me and originally we had lived in Lewes, in Sussex, before moving to Leicester, where my dad was studying art. It was only after his student days were over that we moved to London.

Yep, this was Tottenham. And this was my life. I was very lucky and privileged to be going to one of London's best private schools. I had won a scholarship, thanks to my apparent intellectual capacity. Yet daily I would find myself faced with all sorts of paradoxes, not least being ensconced in a world of elite, rich public-school chums and then coming home to poverty. I remember several times when we scrabbled in the cracks of the floorboards and down the side of the sofa to retrieve coins so we could buy dinner.

Even when we moved to Islington (actually Newington Green, more Hackney than Islington), these issues reared their heads every day. I would find myself being invited to parties and bar mitzvahs at friends' houses in Hadley Wood or Chelsea, resplendent with pools and jacuzzis, cadging lifts off of parents in their Rolls-Royces and Mercedes. Then I would come home, take off my Nike trainers (which Mum would have bankrupted herself to get so I was at least deemed vaguely 'cool') and wistfully dream I had a life like those of my schoolmates.

And so it went, throughout my school years. It wasn't a hard upbringing. No grief, really. I would encounter far worse in later years. And my mum did her utmost for my two sisters and me. As I got older, I found Saturday jobs and holiday jobs. At the point when I was doing A levels, I had found a great group of mates and I spent a lot of time doing all the normal sorts of stuff you do when you are in your late teens. I smoked, had sex, did drugs, got drunk, got mugged – the usual things.

I think my ability to conform at school and get on well with boys who were, for the most part, very well off, coupled with the survival instincts I developed on the streets of Tottenham and Newington Green (many times on the way home I hid in doorways, scared that a group of local lads would spot me in my 'posh' uniform), allowed me to interact really well with most people. I'm sure it was a contributing factor to my being good at my job later in life. But it also meant I was something of an outsider, never really belonging to any particular group, with little sense of identity.

I had a particular aptitude for languages (Russian and French in particular) and, after my A levels, I enrolled at the grandly named University of London School of Slavonic and East European Studies. I had a whale of a time while I was there, as one should do. I never really went to many of my lessons and spent a substantial amount of time in the college bar, which, with its Slavic bent, served a wide variety of Soviet bloc vodkas. The appeal of this routine, however enjoyable it was at first, rapidly waned, and, regrettably, I soon became bored and yearned for some adventure. So, in a moment of youthful impetuousness, I ditched university to go and work at Disneyland in Paris when it first opened in 1992.

I spotted the ad in the *Standard* and bowled up to the interview in Bayswater not knowing what was going to happen. I had no idea what sort of interview to expect or what sort of job I would get. I thought it would be a quick interview, then a letter in the post a few weeks later.

About ten minutes after I arrived, I was talking to a recruiter. They tested my level of French (although, surprisingly, fluent French was not a requirement) and ten minutes after that I was walking out with a permanent employment contract, on 6,500 French francs a month, with a start date five days hence.

Living and working in France was a carefree existence. It was like university but without the study. I had a great time. I had been in France for about six months when I met Jane. We started seeing each other and returned to the UK, where I worked in a series of dead-end jobs, with no career ahead of me and no real ambitions. I was happy to work in a pizza restaurant in Oxford Street, earning terrible money for long hours and coming home smelling of burnt cooking oil and the body odour of the fat Turkish head cook, which permeated every square inch of the kitchen.

While I never felt like I was being a bit of a waster, I'm sure my mum thought otherwise. I could often see the dismay in her eyes when I wandered in, stinking of pizza fat, after a 12-hour shift feeding tourists in Oxford Street.

I would often think that I needed some sort of catalyst to kick me up the arse and motivate me to get a real job.

Lo and behold, Jane fell pregnant in 1994, and I knew it was time to grow up, be responsible and get a decent occupation – something with career prospects, but also something vaguely cool. I was worried that I was far too immature to be a dad. I think I still am, to be honest. I still haven't really grown up at all and am prone to childish sulks and inexplicable infantile behaviour, which often causes upset or annoyance. At the time, I supposed that if I got a 'grown-up' job then I would automatically become a responsible adult.

Jane's family had a strong background in the police. Her uncle worked for the Met in Royalty Protection. He carried a gun. Now that was more like it! How cool was that? Little did I know that the reality of his job was dull, with little or no chance of any interaction with the public and certainly no opportunities to shoot a gun, aside from in the annual shooting test. The closest he would come to an arrest in that role was a cardiac one.

I began to research a career in the police, mainly via ITV's *The Bill*, harbouring dreams of becoming part of PT17, the Firearms Unit, which is now SCO19, rolling over bonnets in blue coveralls and a gas mask, brandishing a machine gun and taking down violent crims. Yes, this was for me. Thanks to my childhood diet of cop shows (especially *CHiPs*) and my new penchant for having a gun, I applied for the Metropolitan Police, my local force.

The application procedure took longer than 18 months. In that time, I went to the gym regularly, desperate to pass the strict fitness test that was in place at the time, and gazed at passing cops and police cars with envy. I read a lot – this was before such luxuries as the Internet – and in particular I consumed books about the police (favourites being *Talking Blues* by Roger Graef and *Watching the*

Detectives by Andrew Brown). Reading these books actually made me somewhat apprehensive. I had never found myself in a testosterone-filled environment where the power of violence ruled over all. I was a meek, mild-mannered ex-public schoolboy and had butterflies at the thought of encountering a violent prisoner or being the victim of some of the initiation pranks reserved for probationers at many London police stations.

I was keen, however, to get out of this typecasting as a posh, intelligent public schoolboy. It was always something I was uncomfortable with, especially because I'm not even that posh. Motivated by an odd desire to be seen as a bit more 'blue collar', as well as the need to support my family, I waited until finally a letter arrived with a date for the interview and the dreaded fitness test.

When the day came, I went to Hendon Police College and was overwhelmed at the prospect of joining the assembled recruits, looking smart and official in their newly issued blue serge uniforms. Some of the recruits swaggered proudly through the school, having been issued with their long acrylic batons and handcuffs worn overtly (an innovation at the time). I definitely wanted to be part of this!

I passed the fitness test – just. I managed the 40 push-ups in a minute, unbelievably. I did, I am proud to report, get one of the lowest ever recorded scores on the 'stretch test'. I have never been the most nimble.

After the fitness tests, all the candidates were interviewed one by one by a panel of senior police officers. My interview seemed to go swimmingly. We were all told not to leave, as we were to find out before the end of the day whether we had made it or not. I ended up being told last, as I lived in central London. After waiting for an hour in a cold, nicotine-stained room, I was informed I had passed and would soon be offered a date to start training at Hendon.

I was overjoyed. Nervous, too. I mean, it was a lot of responsibility being a cop. People's lives could potentially depend on you. Watching episodes of *The Bill* on telly, I would gulp and think, 'Oh my God, I might have to save someone's life or tell them what to do in an emergency.' I didn't necessarily think I would be able to do it.

Being a new dad had given me a bit of the maturity I thought I needed. It was challenging, tiring but ultimately rewarding. I have the privilege of writing this book now as a new dad again, so the sense of awe and the innate knowledge that someone little is depending on you are still very vivid to me. I'm pretty sure that while being a dad was the catalyst for my applying for the police it was also the driving force behind my being a decent policeman in the future. You very quickly learn the arts of patience, diplomacy, communication and the ability to continue working after very little kip.

Yes, I was overjoyed. I could be settled now, knowing I had a job. That's all I saw it as at the time. Certainly at no point did I ever think that I would make it a career. My grand plan was to do my two years' probation and then apply for the armed response teams. In two years, I would be living the dream. Or maybe I'd do some work for Special Branch, combating Russian spies. How little I knew about the workings of the Met. I expected to be in the police for about five years tops. I knew I got bored easily and would doubtless want a change before long.

Oh, how wrong I was.

2
TRAINING DAYS

HENDON TRAINING SCHOOL IS A SOULLESS PLACE, ironically not unlike some of the local authority housing estates we would patrol after graduating. Sombre tower blocks loom over a bleak playing field, with smaller squat buildings beside the running track and roads. These housed, among other things, the gym, pool and Detective Training School, now unfortunately renamed 'Crime Academy'.

With only a little cash in my pocket, and with my other half and baby son up north while I was training, I had made it to Hendon. Quickly, I established friendships with classmates, and I threw myself into it. I'm not going to reveal details of the training, but I was surprised by how much fun it was. From the outset, I warmed to the tasks and enjoyed the role-plays and the interactions with 'baddies'.

I was also surprised by the effortless way I assimilated to the policing aspect of the training. By this I mean the culture of the service. I'd always considered myself a free spirit, someone with a liberal outlook on life and not one to easily conform to authority. At Hendon, however, I quickly understood that once you join the police it becomes your life. Together with the other recruits, I swiftly got into it. Everyone conforms to the ideas of shiny shoes, cropped hair and the chain of command. It's drummed into you from the start.

Despite my enjoyment, 20 weeks is a long time and I was glad when the process was over and I received the news that I'd passed.

I requested a posting to West End Central division because I believed, foolishly as it turned out, that it took in Oxford Street, would therefore be swarming with tourists and my language skills would be put to good use. West End Central, I quickly discovered, did not in fact cover Oxford Street but was based at Vine Street nick, just off Piccadilly, while the big station at Savile Row was being refurbished. Yet, while London's shopping Mecca might not be on my patch, I could still look forward to patrolling bustling Coventry Street, Piccadilly and Regent Street, amongst others.

While I'd been completing the training, I hadn't really spared much thought to what it would actually mean to be a police officer. I harboured few aspirations other than to wander around in my uniform. When the time came for me to start the job for real, I felt anxiety building for the first time. I started to think about the situations I could find myself in and when I contemplated the responsibility I was facing I began to feel quite scared. Somebody's life could be in my hands. I might be required to give them cardiopulmonary resuscitation (CPR). It was something we'd covered extensively in training, but if it came to it on the job would I be up to the task? The more I pondered it, the more convinced I became that I would be absolutely shit as a police officer. Self-doubt plagued me. Was I cut out for this? I'd jumped into the force because I thought the security was the best thing for my young family, but only now did I begin to realise what I was getting myself into. Could I talk someone down from a building safely? Could I calm a volatile situation or use the necessary force to restrain an aggressive villain? I had no idea, but the thought terrified me.

As my first day on the job approached, I knew there was no turning back. But I had no idea what to expect.

From the moment I walked through the doors, I could sense Vine Street police station was a real old nick. From the outset, I encountered fat sergeants smoking pipes, leather-jacket-clad detectives with roll-ups on the go and haggard police constables cursing the radio systems or the state of the antiquated vehicles. There were some proper experienced coppers there, many with more than 20 years on the force, and some of them were truly fearsome.

My first ten weeks were spent on street duty, accompanied by a tutor at all times. My fellow probationers and I were easily recognisable as rookies (as newbies still are today) by virtue of our shiny new black Hi-Tec Magnum boots, various belt pouches and nylon utility belts. At training, we'd heard clichéd stories about the drivers of the area car or station van having their own table in the canteen. Quickly, I discovered the stories were true. Woe betide any of us if we sat there, or even had the audacity to speak to them. It was very old school. The internal politics at the station did nothing to calm my fears. It all seemed like a world that I had no right to inhabit.

At the end of any new recruit's probation, the inspector is supposed to call them in and give them feedback on how they have performed. My inspector was called Paul and from my first impressions I thought he was a good guy. He was always smoking; this, of course, was back in the day when you could smoke in police stations. He always used to wear his hat right at the back of his head.

When it was time for me to be confirmed as a constable, he called me in for my report. I entered somewhat nervously. He was sitting with his tie off, his feet on the desk, the customary cigarette hanging from his lips, his hat cocked as usual on the back of his head.

'You all right, Christian?' he said. 'How you finding it?'

'Yes, it's all right, guvnor.'

'All right. Nice one. Off you go.'

That was it.

I'd soon realise that Paul never praised or conversed with you for the sake of it, but if you needed a bollocking he would give you one. The less he said, the better. It meant he liked you.

I had made it through my probation, but, starting the job proper, I was full of nerves and apprehension. And what I feared most on the streets was confrontation.

There wasn't much chance of encountering any drama to begin with anyway, though. My team worked 'earlies', 'lates' and 'nights'. While I was the probationer, or 'probby', I was expected to do all the shit jobs: make tea for everyone, make toast on Sundays, take the crap calls (the overdoses, the boring crime reports, the mind-numbing security patrols). Although these jobs were dull and routine, it was a good way to cut my teeth.

I cringe at the stupid things I did during those first couple of months, like not listening to the instructions coming over the radio and therefore not being able to tell the driver where we were supposed to be going. It sounds pathetic and insignificant, but small mistakes like that can cause major problems. I was lucky we were not in an emergency situation when my blips occurred.

Those first few weeks also helped me acclimatise to the culture. It was evident that you had to prove yourself on the team before you were accepted, but, in the absence of anything challenging, it was hard to see where the opportunity would come from. As I sat with the more experienced officers in the smoke-filled canteen, I listened to tales of fighting drunks, hitting berserk shoplifters and tackling knife-wielding robbers. It seemed a world away from what we'd learned at Hendon. It could have been bravado, but I suspected that the reality of street policing was far removed from what they taught in training. I knew that if I was going to earn the respect of my colleagues then I too would have to administer some sort of violence, perhaps whether the recipient deserved it or not.

Now, I am not a fighter. I abhor violence and have always ducked away from confrontation rather than meeting it head-on. Even when I was armed with a big stick in the police, I was still utterly frightened at the prospect of getting assaulted or being in a fight. However, it wasn't long before I found myself in the middle of an incident that went some way to showing me the power of a story in the Old Bill.

I was on duty one night when a fellow probby called Bob came on the radio for a van. He had nicked a stroppy drunk in Soho. I was the passenger in the van, tasked with doing anything that didn't involve actually driving it, including getting out and putting prisoners in the back. We pulled up in a rainy Rupert Street, causing a huddle of smackheads to scurry away. I spotted Bob attempting to drag a large bearded chap, who was shouting and being obstreperous, towards us. Without giving it too much thought and with no fear or apprehension, I got out of the van, grabbed the drunk by the arm and took him down to the ground, kneeling on him and slapping my

31

cuffs on him. It was exactly what we'd been instructed to do in training when dealing with difficult customers.

Bob, an ex-army chap, was obviously impressed and by the time I got back to the canteen later that night I was being applauded for my fighting spirit.

'Well done, son,' said one of the more seasoned officers. 'Bob says you floored his prisoner. Stroppy fucker deserved it too, I hear.'

'Yeah, apparently he was proper kicking off,' said another. 'Lucky you were there. Bob says it was a good takedown.'

I'd been fairly blasé about the whole thing, but that incident was to have a marked effect on my standing at the station. Suddenly, I was accepted into the fold and was part of the team. No longer was I addressed as 'boy' and no longer was I expected to do all the dirty work. I was blooded into the force. Over the next couple of weeks, the story of how I'd restrained the old drunk grew arms and legs. In the telling of the tale, I had jumped him and cuffed him on my own, but not before I'd given him a few digs for good measure. It had been nothing like that, but that's how stories develop and I quickly realised it wasn't in my interests to set the record straight. It is quite incredible how a story in the police can develop from truth to fantasy in the space of a few conversations. In the eyes of the old-timers, I had come of age and could be trusted in a scrap. It was a watershed moment. From that point on, I began to relax and got into the way of crime-fighting.

Practically overnight, I went from being an introverted probationer to an assertive uniformed street cop. I started loving the job too, much to my surprise. Gone were my lofty desires to become a gun-toting SO19 stalwart; instead, I was happy being with my team, working day in and day out with people for whom I would gladly have given my life. It might sound quite naive and idealistic, I know, but that was how I felt about the job. I loved it.

I started spending a lot of time patrolling Soho. Before finding my feet, I had stuck rigidly to the safe streets of Mayfair, but my newfound confidence meant I now enjoyed chasing thieves, fighting drunks and skulking around Soho's myriad backstreets searching out the baddies. I had some fantastic experiences, and my eyes were opened to the unbelievable and sometimes astounding situations people got into and the worlds they lived in. Whores, pimps, junkies, crackheads, smackheads, the homeless, drunks, vagrants, dealers, illegal immigrants, minicab drivers, skankers, touts, trannies – you name it, Soho had it.

One night, I was doing my usual rounds when I came across a couple getting it on rather roughly in a doorway in Romilly Street. Only when I pulled them apart did I realise that it was a bloke and a transvestite. He had been taking her up the tradesman's entrance. What was more astonishing was that the man had thought he'd been shagging a woman. The look of horror on his face when I broke the news to him that he'd been indulging in gay sex was a sight to behold.

Not long after that, I stumbled across a smackhead in Dufours Place who was injecting heroin into the base of his flaccid, rotten penis. On another occasion, a crackhead desperate not to lose his last rock threatened me with a knife. Actually, that type of thing became quite commonplace.

Fights, chases, accidents, stabbings, shoplifting, burglaries and thefts from cars were run of the mill. Italian pickpockets, North African bag thieves, Kosovan street traders, Somali taxi touts, Chinese street gamblers, Jamaican crack dealers and many more completed a heady yet seedy multinational mix of criminals who frequented the streets of Soho. I became very fond of the area and it will forever have a special meaning in my life; it's certainly a place that gets into your blood.

I soon gained a reputation as a solid copper, a 'thief-taker', with natural policing ability. I will always remember being in the radio control (or CAD) room at West End Central a couple of years after we moved from Vine Street to Savile Row when Steve, a very experienced, world-weary policeman with years of service, told me in his East End twang, 'You're a good copper you are, Christian.' I was flushed with pride as I modestly batted away the compliment. I have to admit that I had a pretty outstanding arrest rate. It was nearly always for good stuff too – never criminalising people who didn't need it. If I stopped some 17-year-old student with a bit of puff (it was resin back then) and he was OK, the drugs would go down the drain and that would be it. But the baddies of Soho would always be coming into the nick with me – for anything I could think of. I went through a phase of arresting crackheads and smackheads over bizarre antiquated park by-laws in St Anne's churchyard in Soho.

If I couldn't get them for drugs, I was sure to be able to get them for 'wilfully fouling a park bench' or 'being in the park in a verminous state'. I found this terribly amusing for some reason.

It was around this time that I earned my first commendation. I took a call that a man had climbed 100 ft to the top of some scaffolding in Haymarket and was threatening to jump. I sat in the passenger seat of the police van, looking up at the guy, his arms outstretched in a crucifixion pose. I thought, 'Oh my God, he's going to jump.'

We got to the building and I ran up with a security guard

to the floor he was on. I got the guard to open the window. I looked out and could see that the man had stepped back from the edge.

'Thank God,' I thought. It seemed to me we had a split second to decide what to do. We could spend all day talking to him, or there was a chance I might be able to cuff him to the scaffolding. I certainly didn't want him to jump. My colleague and I clambered out. He looked at us but before he knew what was happening we grabbed him and cuffed him to the scaffolding. The poor guy had serious mental issues. With the help of the fire brigade, we managed to get him down safely. When the drama was all over, I felt good that I'd been able to resolve the situation peacefully.

As well as enhancing my reputation within the Old Bill, I made a name for myself amongst the local villainy. Soho had a huge crack and heroin market and all the degradation associated with it. It still has, but it's invisible to normal citizens, I think. Only good street cops can see it. Even now, I can tell by the slightest of nuances, gestures, mannerisms or demeanours exactly what someone is up to. A slight, almost indiscernible movement of the mouth and near-imperceptible shift of gaze told me someone had a mouth full of crack cocaine; a quick scan of his surroundings completed in a millionth of a second by a fake-Prada-clad bag thief told me he'd spotted his prey.

Unless you have it, you will never understand it. Denzel Washington's character in the film *Training Day* describes it as 'the magic eye'. I had (and still have) the magic eye. And this is why Steve called me a 'good copper'.

Already the never-ending shift pattern was taking its toll on my personal life. My dedication to the job led inevitably to frequent arguments and intermittent break-ups, but my problems at home did nothing to quell my enthusiasm for the job. On the contrary, I wanted more. I would have been happy to spend my time at work 24/7. I was having a great time and felt a strong sense of service. I was happy making a name for myself, with goodies and baddies, doing 'proper policing'.

After a few years, however, I thought it was time to move on to something better. Lots of mates had left my team, and I thought I had what it took to work in plain clothes, ditch the uniform and maybe, just maybe, become a detective.

3

WATCHING THE DETECTIVES

WEST END CENTRAL HAD WHAT WAS THEN CALLED A 'crime squad', a team of wannabe detectives who dealt with anything and everything. They were the proactive side of the Criminal Investigation Department and I held them in lofty esteem. They wore long hair and leather jackets and never shaved. I didn't dare speak to them – I was a mere uniformed cop, a 'lid' – but I had begun to daydream about joining their ranks.

In those days, there was an unwritten career path to being a detective. You usually had to prove yourself in uniform, join the local crime squad, then work hard and wait to be recommended by the detective inspector for CID training. Unlike in the US, however, becoming a detective is not seen as a promotion, just as a sideways move into a different department. But, if you were wily, you could get to not shave, a prospect that suited my sensitive skin!

My chance came when I was invited to join a small plain-clothes team called the Soho Unit. This opportunity arose solely as a result of my work ethic and good arrest figures. I was pleased that my efforts had been recognised in some way.

Ostensibly, the unit had been set up to deal with the peculiar phenomenon of 'clipping'. This was a particularly brilliant scam conducted by girls who offered punters sex, took their money and then buggered off. A second 'clip girl' would shortly approach the bemused punter, listen to his tale of woe and then extort more cash under the pretence of going to find the original con artist. And so the circle would continue. Obviously, all the girls would be part of the same crew.

The scam should never have worked.

Once she'd got her £200 for full sex, the woman would often give a lame line, like she had to put a deposit on the flat they were going to use because she rented it by the hour. She'd lead the gullible punter to a doorway. Bourchier Street and St Anne's Court were favourites. There the girl would pretend to post the money, saying something like, 'Right, I've put the money in there. That will be ready for us in ten minutes. I'll meet you round the corner.'

That would be it. It was hardly sophisticated. But she'd be off with his 200 quid and he'd never see her again. Often, it was a team of girls working together and another would approach the punter. She'd say, 'You all right, darling?' He'd explain what happened. She'd say, 'I know her. We'll go and find her. I'll have to make a few calls. Give me some money and I'll speak to some people,' or she'd offer him sex and repeat the scam, and it would go on and on.

The girls were invariably rotten-toothed crackheads or wily, haggard, 40-something east London girls – none of them attractive in any way. The blokes who fell for it – and there were scores of them – would often call the police and say they had been robbed. More often than not, they would say five black guys had robbed them with a knife, or come up with other such fantastical stories. I became very adept at reading between the lines and would often shock colleagues who had attended a 'victim' by arriving and aggressively interrogating him, peppering my questions with phrases like 'you are a fucking liar' and 'don't lie to me, you cunt'. Eventually broken, the 'victim' would confess that there was no gang of brigands running around Soho robbing people willy-nilly and admit that, in fact, he had handed over £200 to a roll-up-smoking, pasty-faced crack whore with facial boils and malodorous breath because he thought he was going to get to fuck her up the bum in a urine-soaked alleyway while his wife and kids were at home. As you can tell, I had little sympathy for them. Despite my reservations, however, they were, in a technical sense, victims of a deception, and sometimes blackmail, so we would have to investigate their claims.

I thought the reason we dedicated so many resources to the scam was that the police are obsessed with stats and in Soho a management priority was tackling robbery figures, particularly where someone had used violence. Many of these clip-girl stings would get reported to uniform colleagues as robberies. Even though the victims' claims would border on the fantastical, the crimes would go on the system as robberies and the stats would look outrageous.

Often the victim could be squared up. We would find the girl, get the money and then give it back to him. All done and dusted.

One guy got bombed for tens of thousands of pounds. He lived in America but was in the UK regularly and kept returning to find out what had happened to his cash. Another bloke, from New York, claimed that a man spinning a variation of the same scam had robbed him. I found the culprit and arrested him. He said the American had asked for little boys, which I didn't believe. Nothing happened in the end. The case didn't go to court, but I arranged for the guy to fly to London and make statements and take part in ID parades and all that jazz. He was really grateful. He sent me five NYPD caps as a thank-you gift for doing a thorough investigation. You wouldn't believe the rigmarole that that caused. I had to fill in all sorts of dockets explaining that they weren't a bribe but an unsolicited gift.

Working in this environment brought us into even more contact with drugs and junkies. Our remit was the clip girls, but nearly all our time was taken up with drugs. We were nicking people for supply and possession and even for an offence of 'offering to supply', but that was happening so often, with three or four arrests each day, that eventually we stopped arresting people for it.

Crack and heroin were very new to me. I had no idea about exactly what they were or what they did. Working the streets, especially at night, was an eye-opener, though. You'd stumble across a gaunt, pasty-faced heroin user in a subway with a needle sticking out of his arm, or, post-fix, standing bent at the waist, swaying like a tree in the wind, in a narcomaniacal trance. You'd see crackheads doing what I called 'the crackhead shuffle' – a long time before 'shuffling' was a hip dance craze! – rocking from side to side, eyes whizzing around, jaw clenched, in a world of ecstasy, momentarily forgetting the putrid sores and aching limbs that were their common physical afflictions.

What was overwhelming was that, although I referred to them as 'scumbags' or 'scrotes' (a term coined by US cop writer Joseph Wambaugh, I believe, but in very common usage amongst London police), they were generally fine to deal with. Maybe I was alone in thinking this, but on very few occasions did I have any problems with them, or they with me. I saw them as people with a problem and I think they had a little respect for me because of it.

One guy, a massive 6-ft-plus man mountain, went nuts once in his filthy hostel dorm and began smashing the place to bits. The police, not knowing what to expect, responded in numbers. Before I arrived on the scene, a few officers had tried to reason with him, but their pleas had fallen on deaf ears. I knew the guy from our interactions on the streets and as soon as I spoke to him he heard me out, only because I had treated him affably in the past. It was a very common refrain from baddies in the area as I ended my encounters with them: 'You're all right you are. You're all right.' He came out very calmly, arms outstretched in the international 'arrest me' pose.

So, armed with plaudits from colleagues and scumbags alike, I ploughed onwards.

Even though we were well known in Soho as cops, people would still come up to us and try to sell us drugs. We made very little attempt to be covert. Although we were in plain clothes, we carried our radios and you could see our batons and handcuffs.

Plain-clothes work was an exciting thing to do as a young officer, but it was also quite scary because I didn't have the shield of the uniform. All I had was a tin badge in a wallet. And when you put yourself in a situation you would never go into in a uniform, the adrenalin would be pumping. Often you would be standing amongst a huddle of junkies and listening to them, watching what they were doing. Every day I went out on the streets, there was a high chance of a physical altercation – and it would be with the lowest of the low.

Often I'd see a heroin addict with his little stash in his hand. I'd grab his wrist, but the last thing a junkie wants is for anyone to take his heroin away. He'd fight like a demon to keep it and we'd find ourselves rolling around on the ground. It was a daily occurrence. It was like being in some sort of film and an exciting way to earn a living.

The Soho Unit consisted of just five officers, all on at the same time, with the vast majority of our work at night. We spent a lot of time with prostitutes and clip girls, and listened to their tales of woe. One girl, Erica, was a prostitute whom we ran as an informant for a while. She was young, maybe about 19, and very pretty. I was really quite overwhelmed whenever we met her – sometimes at the flat she used for work. She seemed so innocent and naive. She was an archetypal bimbo, actually. But we always used to chat in the 'waiting area' and she would regale us with stories about her childhood, about going to church and school, and how she wanted to go back home to Ireland. All the while, I could see the huge price list behind her on the wall: 'Blow Job £10 – Straight £20 – Anal £50'.

It was an incongruous clash of cultures – this tragic, sweet girl caught up in this seedy, messed-up world. Her predicament got to me. Eventually, through continued dialogue with her, we managed to persuade her to get out of the game and, when last I heard, she was on her way home to Ireland with the intention of sorting out her life. Erica was one of the few success stories. Too often, the characters we met were beyond saving.

We would deal with anything and everything, and my reputation only grew. Once scared to wander around the dimly lit Soho streets at night, now I happily marauded through the drug dealers and junkies, waving my badge and watching them all run away. I submitted mountains of quality intelligence from registered and, ahem, informal informants. The local intelligence unit began to notice me.

One evening, I got a call from one of the officers in the intel unit, asking me to come to an office on the first floor at West End Central. Bernard was a young constable, blessed with an acerbic wit and an articulacy I had hitherto not experienced in a policeman. He was to become a very dear friend and, at one point in my career, my boss. I met him outside the office, which, unusually, was equipped with a digital lock. A handwritten sign on the door decreed that entry was forbidden.

'Hello, Christian,' he said. 'We need a favour from you if it's OK.'

'Sure,' I said, as Bernard unlocked the door to the office and ushered me in.

I gazed around the tiny room. All over the walls were photographs of baddies, some of whom I recognised from my Soho patrols. One wall was covered with a whiteboard that listed more than 70 names. Shelves of paperwork covered the windows.

'We've been running a covert operation in Soho over the last few months targeting drug dealers,' he said. 'Don't breathe a word to anyone, OK?'

'OK,' I said, somewhat overawed.

'Now, I know you're working nights this week, and we need someone trustworthy to make sure our technical equipment is working all right,' he said.

Wow! I was very impressed, and extremely pleased to have been given such a task. At this stage, the world of undercover policing was completely alien to me. I had no idea exactly what the officers deployed in Soho were doing to target the 70-odd individuals at that point. I decided it was not my place to ask too many questions anyway, and I listened intently to Bernard's instructions. I was still, technically, a 'lid'.

Bernard asked me to go to a local hotel, handing me a key card for a room on an upper floor. He explained that the room contained a large amount of technical equipment and that someone needed to go there at about 4 a.m. to ensure that the mains power for the equipment was switched off.

Bemused yet intrigued, I agreed. Later, in the wee hours, I gingerly unlocked the door to the down-at-heel budget hotel room. The key card clicked and I pushed the door to. Inside the room, which had been emptied of the usual hotel accoutrements, sat a plethora of CCTV monitors, each showing a different viewpoint of some familiar Soho streets. 'Jesus,' I thought. These were all hidden cameras, watching everything. A control panel with two or three joysticks lay in front of the monitors, enabling the user to zoom, tilt and pan at will. A dozen or so video recorders were also wired up to the system, which was squeezed next to a set of bunk beds, covered in bedding and boxes of surveillance logs, radio batteries and empty Lucozade bottles. Enthralled, I switched off the mains power as Bernard had asked. I locked the door and, like he said, never breathed a word to anyone.

It was only later on in my career that the complexity of such an operation dawned on me, and the hard work that must have gone into not only running it but also keeping it a complete secret from cops like me. I'd thought I knew everything going on in Soho. Evidently not.

Around the time of this operation, which for the time being would remain a bit of a mystery to me, it was decided by top brass that the Soho Unit was to be taken into the West End Central Crime Squad, a bigger plain-clothes unit that had a far wider remit, dealing with any crime, particularly street crime, including robbery, burglary and drug dealing. In the crime squad were people who had been doing this type of work for three or four years. They were the type of police I aspired to be. Some had long hair, they didn't shave, they wore scruffy clothes and, ultimately, they were cool.

Given that the stereotypical dress code for a plain-clothes copper – not undercover – was a North Face fleece or jacket, blue jeans and Timberland boots, by comparison these guys were the real deal. One big black guy had little tiny dreadlocks.

For the next year, we joined the bigger team and continued our street work in Soho. Although we now spent 90 per cent of our time in plain clothes, we were still technically uniform cops, not detectives, and every now and then we were required to get back into character as regular constables.

One of these occasions was the Carnival Against Capital riot in June 1999. The day started slowly enough. We assembled at 5 a.m. and were told that the plan was to contain the large numbers of protesters who were gathering at various locations across central London to campaign against capitalism.

Throughout the day, we heard our colleagues were getting attacked. It was somewhat infuriating not being able to respond on your own initiative, as you would have done normally. All resources were directed by a commanding officer, call sign 'Silver'. We moaned, shouted and whinged to our sergeant that we weren't being effectively deployed, but it wasn't until 1 p.m. that we heard the immortal command on the radio: 'From Silver, all units – kit up!' This meant that the whole shebang had gone tits up and we were going to rock it paramilitary style. In front of the picture window of a local Pizza Hut, much to the surprise of the hungry punters therein, we leapt from our van and began getting our riot gear on: pads, guards, gloves; armour, balaclavas and helmets. At last, we were going to help our colleagues. The adrenalin was pumping and you could have filled the petrol tank with testosterone, so fired up were the officers in our little bus.

We drove into the thick of it; a group had gathered at Queen Victoria Street, opposite a Mercedes showroom, near Mansion House. The bus in front of ours ran someone over and the whole place kicked off, with people jumping all over our vehicle. We had to protect the fire brigade, who were coming under fire nearby. They were doing their damnedest to get this buffoon out from under the police bus but were receiving sticks, bricks and bottles for their efforts. Remarkably, with little baton action, we managed to control the situation, but as we retreated back to our bus the mood of the crowd suddenly turned toxic. Before I knew what was happening, I had been separated from the crowd with one other lad. This other chap, Marvin (who would one day be my detective sergeant), and I evidently thought, 'Fuck,' at the same time.

The crowd ceased to act like a bunch of angry individuals and started moving as one. It was terrifying. The mood was now decidedly ugly, and I thought, 'Fuck me, these people actually want to kill me.'

I kept trying to get back to where I thought the bus was. As the crowd moved in from all sides, I was convinced that if they got me I would be dead – they would rip me limb from limb – so I began lashing out, desperately trying to create some space between myself and the front of the crowd. I didn't know who I was hitting. I was very scared. One bloke to my right had a motorcycle helmet in one hand and a crowbar in the other. Before he could swing either in my direction, Marvin, who was to my right, whacked him and he fell to the ground. The rest of my team suddenly rushed in and dragged the guy with the crowbar away, and somehow we got out of there unscathed. The whole incident might have lasted less than a minute, but it was the closest I'd come to being truly terrified on the job.

I remember the next day being at my sister's house, where she was entertaining a typically left-wing crowd of do-gooders, mockneys and elderflower-wine-drinking wastrels. That they were all excusing the violence of the previous day and saying that the police had been heavy-handed infuriated me no end, and still does to this day. How dare those opinionated idiots talk such codswallop? I'd been absolutely bricking it and seriously thought I was going to die.

A year later, the May Day riots of 2000 were equally violent but not as scary, because this time the police were ready for the protestors: not as much off-the-cuff baton action and we were actually impressively organised when corralling the violent elements. By then, though, I was starting to look out of place as a uniformed cop. Before the operation began, we all met at Buckingham Gate to be fed before we got to work – 'operational feeding', it's called – and we must have looked a right mess. We were all really scruffy. One man had his hair back in a ponytail; I hadn't shaved for six days; Big Eddie had dreadlocks. Typical coppers we weren't. I remember standing in the queue for food and an officer from some outpost nick like Bromley looking at us and saying to his boss-eyed chum, 'They'll be the fucking West End Crime Squad, then.' I smirked and thought, 'You're just jealous, mate.'

My journey into the undercover realm was about to begin.

4

STARSKY AND HUTCH

'GET ON THE FUCKING FLOOR!' I SAID, INWARDLY CURSING my 20-a-day smoking habit. Clarence, a malodorous crackhead, was ferocious in his attempts to wriggle free from my bear hug as I tried to drag his wiry frame to the ground.

My colleague Adrian was punching Clarence in the leg, also shouting for him to get on the ground. Clarence, despite the attentions of two officers, was keeping his mouth firmly closed. He was as desperate to hold on to the crack cocaine in his mouth as we were to get it out. He heaved himself away from me as Adrian sideswiped his legs from underneath him. We fell to the ground in a writhing heap, me at the bottom, forced to breathe in the stench of Clarence's sweat-encrusted tracksuit top. Still gasping, I managed to squirm my way onto Clarence's back, attempting to pin him to the ground. Adrian was now kneeling on his head, trying to grab his flailing arms.

'I'll get his arms, you get the gear,' I spluttered to Adrian, grabbing Clarence's wrists while straddling his back.

Adrian nodded in acknowledgement and began forcing the crackhead's mouth open with his radio, simultaneously pressing down on a nerve behind our captive's earlobe – a trick he'd perfected in situations like these – and shouting, 'Spit the drugs out!'

Grappling Clarence's wrists, I managed to fish my handcuffs from the small of my back and scrabbled to get them on.

Mouth dry, and still breathless from the exertion, suddenly I was hit full-on by what felt like a bus. I went flying, handcuffs clattering across the cobbles of Moor Street.

I landed heavily on the roadway and got to my feet, trying to make sense of what was going on. My cuffs had come to rest a few yards away, at the feet of a tourist who I realised was filming everything. Just then, I was grabbed around the upper body from the back and chucked to the ground by an unknown adversary. Out of the corner of my eye, I caught sight of police uniforms and the reflection of blue lights in a shop window.

The officer who had thrown me on the ground now roughly hauled me to my feet.

'I'm job. I'm job, you fucking twat,' I protested, while angrily pulling my warrant card out of my back pocket and brandishing it for all to see.

'Shit, sorry, mate,' he replied. 'We just thought you were fighting with him.' He pointed to a now unmistakably detained Clarence, who by this point had swallowed his stash of crack cocaine. The officer was from the TSG or Territorial Support Group, the Met's riot cops. They didn't know Adrian or me and weren't local to the area, so I could understand why they had intervened in our arrest.

Still, as I glumly wandered over to pick my handcuffs up from the gutter, I heard that Adrian was on the radio asking for an ambulance to take Clarence to hospital. This would mean a lot of paperwork, thanks to the fucking TSG.

The sergeant came over and apologised once again. 'You two look like a pair of fucking crackheads yourselves,' he explained. Only slightly offended, I smiled to myself. With longer hair than allowed, three days' facial growth, leather jackets and dirty jeans, we certainly didn't look like cops.

'It's OK, sarge,' I said to him. 'I'm getting used to that.'

Since I'd teamed up with Adrian, situations like this were becoming commonplace.

I'd first met Adrian while I was still in uniform, before I left to join the Soho Unit. I didn't speak to him much in those days. Adrian was a brash, loud and outspoken Northerner. He disliked complying with authority and was something of a maverick. He seemed arrogant and cocksure, to be honest, but there was something intriguing about him even then. He was in uniform, like the rest of the officers, but he had loads of tattoos – the artwork nearly covered his arms – and he sported spiky hair, unheard of for a cop. In addition, he wore earrings and other jewellery and had piercings all over the place. In a team full of strait-laced, standard-issue coppers, he looked right out of place. Some people thought he looked weird, but he didn't seem to care less. He had about seven years more experience than me and had worked for the Clubs and Vice Unit previously, dealing with prostitutes and young runaways.

Then he came onto the crime squad. We were thrown together and quickly I realised he was actually pretty cool. Little did I know the impact and influence he would have on my career and, eventually, my life. As I got to know him, he seemed like a kindred spirit. I guess, like me, he wasn't necessarily the best copper in the world, but he was hard-working and enthusiastic. He just needed a kick up the arse sometimes to get him properly motivated, and in those days I had built up a bit of a reputation for being an arse-kicker.

When we started working in Soho together, we were very quickly left to our own devices because we used to arrest people on a very regular basis. That might sound strange, because I'm sure people would imagine that arresting people is what cops do for a living, but, believe me, that's not always a given. Lots of cops don't arrest people. Some will even admit it. 'That's not my bag.' Fair enough. Others are just crap at their job. They don't see what good cops see.

Adrian and I, on the other hand, used to charge around Soho like it was our manor. We targeted drug dealers, users, petty thieves and other street criminals. It was often messy. Frequently we'd find ourselves rolling around on the ground with some druggie, trying to seize his stash.

We built up a rapport and an understanding together and, with Adrian's help, I fine-tuned my 'magic eye'. Adrian would rely on me to say who was worth following, who to search. It worked and it was the foundation upon which our reputation was built.

We acted and thought the same and soon we even dressed the same. We eschewed the usual plain-clothes 'uniform' of North Face jackets, pressed 501s and Timberlands in favour of retro Nikes, dirty second-hand jeans and '70s leather jackets. We were usually unkempt and unshaven, and our tools of the trade were radios and 'old-school' chain-link handcuffs. We cultivated informants, ran operations and knew everyone and everything in Soho. We attracted a lot of attention, both within the force and on the street, but it wasn't just for show. It was effective. We were arresting people every day. We became famous – at least in the police station and amongst the local criminals.

In the weeks since Adrian and I had been working together, I'd been rugby-tackled to the ground on several occasions by cops and members of the public alike, under the mistaken impression that I was a villain of some sort. In one incident, I was sprinting down Shaftesbury Avenue chasing some petty crook or junkie and two uniform coppers were running along behind me. I'm sure it would have been a sight reminiscent of a famous picture from *The Guardian* in the 1980s showing a white guy, a black guy and a uniformed copper all running down the street. The common misconception is that the copper is chasing the black guy. In actual fact, he is a plain-clothes cop, chasing the same hoodlum. I was in the process of trying to get on my radio to alert Adrian that I was after someone when a Spanish tourist saw the commotion and thought he would do his civic duty by stopping the thief from getting away. The trouble was he thought the coppers were chasing me and promptly rugby-tackled me to the ground. I ended up in the middle of the street splatted on the ground. The guy we were chasing was long gone. The tourist was extremely apologetic. *C'est la vie.*

Still, that was the price you paid for getting some of the best arrest rates at the nick. Adrian and I were becoming an unstoppable duo. Already, we'd earned the nickname 'Starsky and Hutch' from the local drug-dealing fraternity. We swiftly became firm friends and we did almost everything together, on and off duty. I was happily living out a movie-cop dream!

'Jumping' crack dealers – the phrase we coined for nabbing them before they swallowed their stash – we had down to a fine art. Often these guys would carry anything from five to fifty rocks of crack in their mouth and wouldn't think twice about downing them if jumped on. We devised training on how to get people to open their mouths, by applying pressure, gentle of course, to nerve endings and stuff like that. I named it Narcotics Extraction Techniques. The name never caught on but the tactics did, even if they rarely produced much success.

The targets would always fight and we would come back with cuts and bruises. We couldn't fight like they did, so it could take four of us to bring down one guy. It would always look bad, messy, but the reality was it was safe and controlled. Only Customs had the power to hold someone until drugs passed out of their body, and looking inside a suspect's mouth was deemed an intimate search. For it to work for us – and to make sure we weren't on shaky ground legally – we had to arrest the dealers first and then search them. We were the pioneers, in many ways, and a lot of how drug dealers are handled now is down to what we did back then. It's quite rare now for these guys to keep drugs in their mouths. If they do, they might keep three or four rocks rather than fifty.

On one occasion, we thought we'd lost a guy. I was out in uniform with the superintendent, the chief of the police station. He was a really nice man, very proactive, who loved Adrian and me. We were with a uniformed cop doing the rounds in Soho Square. A black guy walked towards us. He didn't do or say anything. The uniform cop and I looked at each other. We didn't say anything. I knew the man was a drug dealer and I'd have bet that month's wages that he had gear in his mouth. His eyes might have gone in the other direction or his mouth might have twitched, but it was enough for me to suspect something.

He was summarily jumped on. He did have drugs in his

mouth, which he refused to spit out. The trouble was they got lodged in his throat as he tried to swallow them. He started frothing at the mouth and was having difficulty breathing. Very swiftly that difficulty became life-threatening. He stopped breathing. We didn't know what the fuck to do. Luckily, we had called for assistance in the split second before we jumped him. A police car turned up, driven by a guy who also happened to be a medic. He gave him the old Heimlich manoeuvre and 15 lumps of crack came out with a load of vomit. He was ferried straight to hospital.

I can remember the expression on the face of the superintendent. In that moment, he looked as though he could see his career going down the pan before his eyes, all because he thought he'd be one of the boys and go out with these two idiots. The colour drained from his face. He needn't have worried. It all turned out fine.

One evening, at a West End club, Adrian was drunkenly entertaining an assembled group of us with tales of derring-do as a Test Purchase Officer. I had no idea that this sort of activity existed. Adrian explained that a TPO was trained to go out and buy small quantities of drugs from dealers in order to gather evidence to be used in prosecuting them. It was a world shrouded in secrecy and not many people had any knowledge of it. Hearing Adrian tell us about using his wits to buy crack on the streets of north London, or talking his way out of a sticky situation on a gypsy site, I was flabbergasted. He explained that was the reason his tattoos and piercings were tolerated by the top brass. They helped him blend in with the communities he was attempting to infiltrate.

One of the sergeants who was present said to me, 'Christian, you look gaunt and unhealthy like a junkie. Maybe you should do it!' This raised a hearty laugh and was meant as a piss-take. I thought it was a great idea, though, and began to make some tentative enquiries about becoming a TPO. Word was I had to submit an application to a department called SO10, Covert Operations, and then wait for a course.

Adrian explained that they also ran a course, known to be very demanding, for training and selection of undercover officers (UCOs). These were seen as a level above TPOs and operated completely secretly, using different identities, infiltrating gangs, buying guns and large hauls of drugs. He said he was in the process of applying for his UC course.

Enthralled, I knew immediately that I wanted to do this. I was especially keen to do the TP course, as I thought I had a good grounding for it with my keen sense for street policing. Certainly if Adrian could do it, then I wanted to do it too.

I read about SO10 and demanded information about them from experienced detectives at the nick. Few of them knew anything about the department. It was obviously a pretty secret part of the Met. This only served to glamorise it even further in my head.

I searched for information high and low, and eventually found a book about the Met – I think it was called *Scotland Yard* – which had lengthy chapters detailing each department. I remember eagerly scrabbling through the contents and finding the page on 'SO10 – Covert Operations'. Unlike all the other chapters, this one was half a page. It simply said that SO10 was the Met's most secretive unit and was responsible for undercover operations and training. Little else was mentioned. Intriguing stuff! I definitely wanted some of this mysterious secret-squirrel unit.

I spoke to Bernard, who'd given me that job to do for the intel unit in Soho all those years ago. He put me in touch with John, the guy who sorted all the TPOs out and allocated them their operations. After a brief chat, he handed me a docket with 25 pages of forms to fill in. Perusing it for some time, I filled out the lengthy application over a period of weeks, peppering it with jokey anecdotes, bigging myself up and even referring to myself as a 'Soho celebrity'. It was full of verbose waffle, which I thought would impress the SO10 bigwigs.

Satisfied that I had written a top-notch piece of literature, and with my detective inspector's signature on the application form, I eagerly made my way to New Scotland Yard (or 'the Yard' as it is colloquially known). Clutching my application to become a test purchase officer, I felt somewhat important. I made my way to an anonymous corridor on the upper floors and found the discreet entrance to the world I yearned to be part of. A tiny sticker on the door, about the size of a matchbox, simply said 'SO10'. The door, a stable-style one, blocked the entrance to the office, and shouts and laughter could be heard from within. The top half of the stable door was slightly ajar and the bottom half firmly shut. Gingerly, I tapped on the top half of the door. It was flung open by a large, brutish-looking chap with short sandy hair and a mottled face. He looked like he ate little posh cops for breakfast, and he had evidently seen his fair share of violence, with his twisted nose and scarred face.

'What the fuck do you want?' he rasped into my face, not a hint of a jest in his voice.

'Er, I've got my TP application here,' I stammered meekly.

'Give it here.' He snatched it from my grasp and tore open the envelope I had put it in. He read through some of the form, laughing intermittently. He looked at me after a couple of seconds and said, 'OK, you can go now.'

'Oh . . . er, is that it?' I said. I didn't even know who the bloke was. None of the SO10 staff ever wore ID.

'Yep.' And he shut the upper half of the stable door, to a cacophony of laughter from inside the office.

The whole thing had an air of mystery about it. It was obvious that SO10 was a unit like no other and I began to really yearn to join their ranks. Now, I supposed, I just had to wait.

'Bad news, son,' said my DS some days later.

Thinking the worst about my TP application, I said, 'Oh, shit, no. What is it?'

'Your chum is outta here,' he said, nodding towards Adrian, who was across the office, hunched over a computer. 'He's passed his DC's course. He'll be going to another nick soon,' he explained.

I walked over to Adrian. 'What you up to, mate?' I asked.

'Just finishing my UCO application,' he answered. 'There's a course coming up soon and I need to get it done.'

'Oh, cool,' I said. 'And you've passed your DC's as well?'

'Yeah,' he said and looked at me complainingly. 'I'll just get posted to some shithole or other, won't I?'

'Congratulations anyway, brother,' I said. But inside I was sad. I knew it was the end of a great era. Adrian was soon to move to the CID, the main office, investigating major crimes on our manor. No more running round the streets for him.

5

YABLOKI

THE MET HAD A ROVING SQUAD OF DETECTIVES, CALLED SO7 at the time, that visited different high-crime areas of London on a rolling basis to tackle robbery, violence and drug dealing.

A while after I had joined the crime squad, SO7 visited central London for three months of proactive, covert police work. All of us on the crime squad were redeployed to various mini-teams for the duration of the operation. I was assigned to Red Team, which was led by a hard-grafting DC called Craig. He was probably the most 'job-pissed' copper I had ever met, which is to say he was obsessed with work. We got on very well from the off and, after a couple of weeks doing various bits and bobs of surveillance in Soho, Craig organised a test purchase operation to target those dealers who wouldn't succumb to being 'bounced' across the pavement.

This was my first real involvement with anything like this and I was, of course, intrigued and excited, especially as I had my test purchase application in the system.

Craig did all the paperwork needed, set up all the staff, organised a secure location (which was an old police section house in Soho) and got hold of the technical kit we would need. He even ordered a TV, a tea urn and a fridge to ensure that we would all be comfortable during the job. Despite the presence of a couple of DSs and a DI, Craig essentially ran the entire job.

'Bollocks!' shouted Craig. It was a common refrain.

'What's up?' asked Ginger, one of the DSs.

'Bollocks, bollocks, bollocks,' said Craig again. 'Fucking guvnors asking for the world.'

It seemed that drugs operations were not the flavour of the month in central London (they never would be) and Craig was constantly being asked to provide in-depth analyses and the whys and wherefores of mounting a complex covert operation.

'Bollocks!' he shouted. 'It's all bollocks!'

At an informal discussion just before Craig submitted the incredible amount of paperwork required to get the operation up and running, he asked me to give the operation a Russian name – something unusual to make it stand out.

I smiled inwardly and said, 'Yep, I've got it. Yabloki. Operation Yabloki. Sounds good, eh?'

'Yabloki?' mused Craig. 'Yeah, OK. What does it mean?'

'Bollocks,' I said, grinning broadly.

And so Operation Bollocks was born. It amused the team that the highest ranks had sanctioned an operation with a name that was, essentially, a swear word. Luckily, it also meant 'apples' so we had a Get Out of Jail Free card there.

I found myself in a role that would not expose me on the streets during the operation. I was too well known in Soho, so I took responsibility for the exhibits side of things. I had to deploy the TPOs, account for and bag the drugs they bought, give them their buy money, make sure their evidential notes were up to date and do a whole plethora of other things. It meant I was always first in and last out of the 'office'. This was good for my bank account but not necessarily my home life. It was the blueprint for my working life during the next few years.

After all the i's were dotted and t's were crossed, finally we had a go-live date.

'Good afternoon, everyone,' said Craig. 'Welcome to Operation Yabloki.' A few of us sniggered.

'We are all here for the same reason, and I'll go through the operational plan shortly,' he said. 'But I'd like to say thanks to you all for being here: SO7, TSG and the crime squads from West End Central, Charing Cross and Marylebone. And now I'd like to introduce our first couple of TP officers for the operation.'

Craig grandly opened the door to the room – the old TV lounge – and in traipsed Mark and Scotty. I was overwhelmed. These two guys looked utterly like dirty junkies. Mark was actually Mark Kennedy, who went on to be a full-time UC officer and made headlines when details of his infiltration of the environmental protest movement were revealed. Like me, he eventually found his job clashed with his morals. He had unwashed, long blond hair, piercings all over the place and a wonky eye that made him look like he'd walked off the set of *Deliverance*! Scotty was a waif of a man with bleeding facial sores and the lankiest, greasiest hair imaginable. I was later to learn that he inflicted his facial wounds using a cheese grater, sandpaper or a Stanley knife and that the hair grease was a liberal application of coconut oil. Incredible. I was fascinated by these guys and decided I would use my time with them to grill them about being a TPO and the course that I had in my sights.

For three months, night after night, whatever the weather, we sent Mark, Scotty and other TPOs out into the badlands of Soho with hidden cameras and surveillance teams.

I ended up spending a lot of time with Mark in particular and got on really well with the guy. He reminded me a bit of me, actually – fairly idealistic and very articulate. He spoke often of his intention to go on the national undercover course and eventually get into the 'domestic extremism' side of covert policing. He wasn't your run-of-the-mill copper, that was for sure. We got on because we were both seen as slightly odd or abnormal. Whether that was by virtue of dress, language or mannerisms, I don't know, but that was certainly the perception of me, especially after I had partnered up with Adrian. I liked that, though. I enjoyed – and still do enjoy – going against the grain, being a bit different and not necessarily complying with society's expectations all the time.

During the job, I learned a huge amount from the TPOs. They got themselves into a lot of sticky situations – like being asked to place crack or heroin in their mouths – yet managed to wheedle out of them.

I learned how to write a professional set of evidential notes, how to manipulate hidden cameras to get the best view, the most secure way of wearing a wire, how to carry my buy money, how to get a dealer's phone number, how to make copies of my covert video footage, how to write out evidence bags properly. It was an awesome experience, a heady introduction to the world of TP operations.

Because Craig ran the show so professionally, we would have thorough briefings and debriefings (later in my career, I ran my own TP jobs in the exact same manner) and discuss any issues.

'Yeah, bit of a problem, Craig,' said the TSG sergeant.

'What the fuck have you lot done now?' groaned Craig.

'Well, we jumped on Sean last night, didn't we?' said the skipper. 'You said there was intel to suggest he was hiding crack in his false left arm?'

'Er, that's right,' said Craig.

I knew Sean was a prolific Jamaican crack dealer who, despite having a false arm, would often fight to get away when stopped. Most times, his arm would fall off too and you would have nowhere to put the second handcuff!

'Well, he fought like a bastard last night and his arm fell off.' There were some laughs. 'So we told him, after we searched him, that we would take the arm to the nick and he could have it back today,' continued the sergeant.

'OK. Where's this going exactly?' asked Craig.

'Well, unfortunately, Dingo over there,' he said, nodding to one of his troops, 'put the arm in the DNA freezer overnight.'

There were hoots of laughter, some almost hysterical.

'And Sean came to pick it up an hour or so ago – I'm afraid he's put in a formal complaint to the duty officer saying his arm is frozen solid!'

The room was in stitches.

'In addition,' said the skipper, 'the paperwork has your name all over it, so it's your complaint.'

Craig looked disbelievingly at the sergeant. 'You wankers. You fucking idiots. I'm gonna get a complaint from a one-armed Jamaican crack dealer saying his fucking false arm is frozen solid?'

'What a load of bollocks, eh, Craig?' someone said gleefully.

'Yes, bollocks,' said Craig, the slightest trace of a grin on his face.

After three months, we had got enough evidence against more than thirty drug dealers. The TSG officers in our little team now went into full swing for the arrest phase. This meant scouring the streets for our targets, or getting the TPOs to call them to come onto the 'plot', or area of operations, so the rufty-tufty TSG could do a 'take-out' or 'bounce' them. We had fitted covert cameras in the places where most of our dealing took place and I had the pleasure of watching on camera with the TPOs as all of their targets got taken down by officers of the TSG van.

It was apparent to me that the eventual arrests of these dealers gave the TPOs a substantial amount of satisfaction, after all the efforts they had gone to, the hours they had worked – in all weathers and dealing with the lowest dregs of society – and the risks they had taken. It seemed that it was a fitting end to a lot of hard work for them.

I had made up my mind: I hoped I got a TP course soon; I wanted to do what they did.

Some time after the end of Operation Yabloki, my Nokia buzzed into life as I sat in our office with piles of prosecution requests in front of me. It was Adrian. He was doing his national undercover course, so I answered eagerly, hoping for a full rundown of the ins and outs of the secret mob.

'They're complete cunts,' said Adrian. I could sense the emotion in his voice.

'Oh, shit,' I thought.

'Well, it's their loss, mate,' I consoled him.

'And they had a right go about my tattoos,' he said. 'Make sure you never go on that fucking course with tattoos. They are a complete bunch of wankers.'

I began to think that I wouldn't go on the course at all. It sounded like a fucking nightmare. Adrian had been summarily chucked off the national undercover course after the first week. He had put his heart and soul into preparing for it and he was totally set on becoming a UCO. With no reason given, he was off. No explanation – just quietly removed from the course and sent back to West End Central CID.

Adrian was a good guy, but his extrovert nature probably played some part in his removal from the course. I had heard that you were expected to keep your gob shut and take the criticism on the chin. I couldn't imagine Adrian doing that.

A couple of weeks later, he was transferred to Fulham CID to pursue his detective career. When you stop working with someone constantly, it becomes difficult to stay in touch. Of course, we kept in contact as far as possible, but our paths went in slightly different directions, and Adrian eventually left the police, got married to his beautiful wife, Karen, and moved to Australia.

I didn't know it then, but I would spend the rest of my career trying to find the same sense of belonging, the same satisfaction and the same status that I had enjoyed when we were the Starsky and Hutch of Soho. I tried to find a new Adrian. Sometimes I almost succeeded, but it was never quite the same. I missed working with him and missed the brotherhood we had; we shared so many ridiculous experiences, in and out of work.

Somewhat disheartened, but nonetheless keen to work as usual, I continued my efforts, with my eye still on pursuing my desire to get into the SO10 realm.

Some months hence, nattily clad in my second-hand Savile Row three-piece suit and Paul Smith brogues, I grinned as the Tube train trundled towards Colindale and the foreboding tower blocks of Hendon training school came into view.

Nervous but also excited, as the train ground to a halt

I mentally prepared myself for the week ahead. Breezing through the barrier and meandering towards the training school, I lit up my umpteenth fag of the day and glanced at my watch. 'Shit,' I thought, 'I'm late.' Soles clumping along the pavement, I began running.

After a fair amount of time, I had been allocated a place on a test purchase course. If I was successful, and it was a big if, I could follow in Adrian's footsteps and spend my time getting paid to buy drugs. It was all I wanted to do. Before I got to that stage, however, I had to negotiate the course.

There were dozens of myths surrounding it. For a start, it was said to be ridiculously difficult, with a failure rate of about 50 per cent. I did have one thing going in my favour, though. This was to be the first (and last) non-residential TP course, which meant we had the luxury of being at the training school from 8 a.m. to 6 p.m., as opposed to the normal scenario where the students stayed overnight every night for a week. They would be expected to ingratiate themselves with the instructors, who were all experienced UC officers from the SO10 office, by staying up all hours drinking after class.

Puffing and panting, I bumbled into the classroom about two minutes late, much to the annoyance of the DS instructor. I breathlessly apologised and took my seat in the semicircle of chairs, my name already plastered to the attached folding desk. As I clattered noisily into the chair, dropping my kitbag full of filthy junkie clothes to be used in the role-plays, the instructor, a swarthy, Mediterranean-looking chap called Anthony, said, 'Sit the fuck down, please.'

Nervous and clumsy, I mumbled another apology and pulled myself together as he began his course introduction again.

'Brrrrrrring . . . Brrrrrrring . . .'

'Shit, shit, shit,' I thought.

Yes, I had forgotten to switch my phone off. Bollocks. Like a complete idiot, I scrabbled around in my pockets, desperately trying to silence the blasted thing. Eventually, I found it, my face reddening, sweating profusely. I hurriedly removed the battery and apologised sheepishly to Anthony, whose face was like thunder.

My card was marked. At the time, although I was embarrassed, I thought that at least they'd noticed me. Fool.

So, with the instructors now firmly focused on me, the interrogation began. Not one to let myself come across as a complete dickhead just once, I told the instructors that I absolutely loved giving evidence at Crown Court, that I considered it like a game of chess against the defence and all that sort of nonsense. I thought maybe that was what they wanted to hear, but comments like that only served to enhance their view of me as a gobby, posh twat.

Throughout the course, we were exposed to dozens of role-plays designed to throw us out of our comfort zones, to test our knowledge of drugs and case law. The role actors were all experienced TPOs and gave us a bloody hard time. I was subsequently to do exactly the same on dozens of TP courses in the future.

The course was loosely based on the undercover course, as almost all of the same rules and regulations applied. It was apparent, though, that the SO10 instructors considered TP officers to be second-class citizens in the covert-policing world. Passing the TP course would never be enough to gain credibility with the SO10 elite.

I floundered in some of the role-plays and I was convinced that I would get chucked off halfway through the course. By some massive stroke of luck, however, I made it through to the end. I'm pretty sure that someone, possibly Craig, who was role-acting on the course, put in a good word for me. It was hard, but all of us students at least knew we had had a right result by getting a non-residential course. It was nowhere near as intense or exhausting as the usual week-long nightmare on which I was to assist many times in the future.

One of the final exercises was the court role-play, where we had to give evidence in a mock court based on the notes we had made during one of our role-plays. I had totally forgotten the comment I'd made at the beginning of the course about 'loving to give evidence' as I sat with my assembled fellow students in the 'public gallery' awaiting our turn in the witness box, with the instructors playing the parts of the judge, prosecution and defence. Oddly enough, it was Anthony who would be grilling us as the defence lawyer.

One by one, the ten remaining students (we had started with sixteen) got up and gave evidence. None of it was challenging and each student spent an easy five minutes in the box. Slowly, it dawned on me that Anthony was leaving me till last and evidently had a 'special' line of questioning planned.

I wasn't wrong. All rules went out the window as I stepped into the box. I was there for around two hours batting off Anthony's ridiculous line of questioning.

'Officer, is it true that you are a "celebrity" in Soho?'

Bound by the oath I had sworn, I couldn't lie. To do so would mean dismissal from the course. No one wants a perjurious officer in a covert role.

'Er, sort of,' I said.

'Sort of, eh?' Anthony continued. 'And did you "sort of" buy drugs from my client? Did you "sort of" recognise him from previous dealings? Did you "sort of" put the drugs in an evidence bag when you got back to your secure location? "Sort of", officer?'

'Christ,' I thought. 'Whatever I say, I'm gonna get creamed.'

'Officer,' asked Anthony. 'Do you know Adrian W.?'

Unsure about this, I nonetheless answered, 'Yes.'

'And is it true that he recently attended the national undercover course?' he asked.

'Shit,' I thought, 'we're not supposed to divulge any of this sort of stuff.'

'Er, I refuse to answer that question as it may prejudice covert policing operations,' I pleaded to the judge, a football hooligan of a man with a shaved bonce and gold sovereign rings on every finger.

'Answer the question, please,' demanded the judge.

'Er, yes, I think so,' I whispered.

'And is it true that he called you after this course and referred to the instructors as "cunts"?' asked Anthony, as the remaining students cracked up laughing.

'Er, I don't know,' I said.

'How the fuck do they know that?' I thought.

'Hmm. You don't know much, do you, officer?' asked Anthony.

And so it continued, for two hours, questions that had no basis in reality and would never, ever have been asked in a real court case. The object was to make me feel completely uncomfortable. This was simply payback for me being a cocky upstart and for having the effrontery to say I 'loved' giving evidence. This was the way of SO10.

Still, I didn't break down and managed to handle myself with a fair degree of aplomb, so much so that as I stepped down from the box, exhausted, I received a polite round of applause from my student colleagues.

Shortly afterwards, and two coffees and six fags later, we were gathered in the classroom and told that we had passed the course. High fives all round. The relief was overwhelming; you could almost hear the pressure leaving people's bodies. I knew deep down that somehow I had passed and it was almost definitely thanks to someone I knew 'having a word'. I never felt 100 per cent like I deserved to pass, to be honest.

John, the test purchase liaison guy who gave us our work, popped in, took our numbers and said we'd get a call when some work came up. Happily, we all trooped out and down to the pub for celebratory drinks.

Only a week later, I was called by John, who, in his delightfully friendly soft Scottish brogue, said, 'Christian, Ah've got a little jobbie for you in Tottenham if you're available.'

'Shit. This is it,' I thought. Butterflies in my stomach.

And so was born one of my most often-used phrases: 'Of course, John. Of course I'm available!'

6

BACK TO TOTTENHAM

I WANDERED INTO THE LITTLE NORTH LONDON POLICE station, nervous and worried. I introduced myself to a gruff detective sergeant, who looked me up and down and asked me if it was my first job. I meekly replied, 'Yes,' and he showed me into the drug squad 'office'. Assembled there were about 35 officers. All eyes were on me as I hoisted my bag (with my TP kit inside) onto my shoulder and went into a small anteroom, where I had been directed to get changed.

I was absolutely shitting myself, on the verge of vomiting. I shakily got changed and did my soon-to-be-perfected TP make-up routine. Grabbing a smelly fleece jacket from my bag, I returned to the busy and noisy briefing room and sheepishly sat at the front near the DS.

'Right. Chris is our TP tonight,' said the gruff detective sergeant, waving a hand at me. 'Chris. Stand up, please.' The hubbub died down.

I stood up and half-waved to the officers in front of me at the briefing. I was slightly embarrassed by my filthy clothes, made-up face (bags under the eyes, sores on the mouth and grotty, grimy fingernails) and fake nose and ear piercings.

The DS explained our objective: to buy crack and heroin from a Somali gang in West Green Road in Tottenham. They were, in fact, operating only 20 yards from the house where I'd grown up.

With seemingly a million things to think about (notebook, phone, recording device, safety signals, people to target, location of the plot, money to buy drugs), I prepared myself to hit the streets of Tottenham, not as a blazer-clad public schoolboy this time but as a cop pretending to be a crackhead. I left all my real-life stuff (warrant card, wallet, etc.) behind at the nick and became an identity-less drug user.

An hour later, my hands shaking with nerves as I chain-smoked cigarettes, I wandered (nonchalantly, I thought) down West Green Road. Even though it was dark, the street was busy, and the 'magic eye' kicked in: I could easily identify those who looked like they were 'serving up'. I approached a group of Somalis and, adopting the ridiculous false 'London youth' accent (which was to become the bane of my life), I cautiously asked if 'anything was about'.

The apparent ringleader, who couldn't have been more than 15 years old, looked me up and down and simply said, 'Fuck off, officer.'

I laughed, nervously, and tried to remonstrate: 'But, I'm not –'

He exploded, 'Listen, white boy – fuck off,' and laughed. One of his chums spat on the ground. Feigning anger, I walked off, away from the group, kicking a rubbish bag into the road in an apparent fit of pique.

Inside, I was wondering and fretting. Did they recognise me? Is my fakery too obvious? Do I sound too much like a cop? Don't I look enough like a crackhead? Can they see in my eyes that I'm lying? Can they see I'm a cop?

I bought a beer to settle my nerves and began to simply wander up and down for half an hour. Eventually, I was approached by a young Somali lad who sold me what he claimed was crack for £25. Thinking I had scored, I was fairly chuffed and triumphantly returned to the police station.

First, I had paid well over the odds for one rock and, second, I hadn't taken time to check what it was. That was to prove costly. It hadn't been crack he sold me – it was chewing gum!

The next evening, I returned (having spent the day doing my normal day job in the CID at West End Central). We went through the same briefing and I did exactly the same, only this time I was hunting for the guy who sold me the chewing gum, in order to front him out and have a go at him for 'skanking' me.

I never found him and spent around six weeks going to and fro along West Green Road, often being told to fuck off, or getting skanked with chalk or paracetamol. It was a steep learning curve.

I was desperate to succeed, but I started to notice that every time I went out on a TP job I developed a horrific headache. They would build with the anticipation of the task ahead and only subside once the job was over or if I realised the night wouldn't be as stressful as I'd feared. Sometimes I'd be out for five minutes; sometimes it would be five hours. During this time, I discovered that my capacity for pretending to be someone else in a stressful situation was quite limited. It wasn't that the job was particularly stressful; I was making it so. I was always thinking, 'What if he knows I'm a copper?'

Just as cops could have the magic eye, baddies, I believed, had the same ability to sniff out who was a copper. Was I giving away a telltale sign? It might have been something subtle that I'd done, like going for where my handcuffs would normally be under my belt, and they'd spotted that. Or did I touch my ear or pat where my recording device was for reassurance? Did my eyes give me away? I was sure criminals could detect when someone was scared, as opposed to desperate, like most junkies. These were people who would have no qualms about killing someone they thought was a snitch, or punching or stabbing someone they didn't like the look of.

Controlling my fear was a constant battle for me.

Perseverance paid off, however, and I eventually managed to get into the exact group of young Somalis who had rebutted me many nights before. Lo and behold, the ringleader, who had been so vociferous that first evening, was now giving me his phone number while selling me heroin for £15 a bag (usual price a tenner; the fiver was obviously his commission).

I was overjoyed and got a fantastic buzz from buying it. It was pure and simple front-line policing. Not even front-line, in fact; it was behind enemy lines! I loved it. What a great rush!

Over the course of four or five months, I returned to be deployed dozens of times, each time buying crack or heroin and helping to identify dealers, venues and stash locations – all on top of my normal CID workload. In a pattern that would repeat itself with every new test purchase job, I was working around 70 hours a week. The money was a bonus, but at the time I did it because I loved doing it. I found it cool, glamorous and exciting.

All good operations must come to an end, however, and all the dealers were picked up on a grand 'arrest day'. Because I was essentially undercover, I obviously didn't get involved in all of that. This was the good thing about being a TPO. You had an air of mystery about you. We would turn up, no one really knew who we were, and we would buy drugs, gather evidence and then go home. It would be up to the operational team to do all the hard graft, putting cases together and arresting the baddies.

Young and full of vigour and enthusiasm, I couldn't wait for my next task. It couldn't come soon enough. My CID job was getting staid and boring. And I disliked my boss. I had once walked out of the CID office on my way to execute a search warrant wearing my body armour, which was decorated with an image of Jesus in Russian Orthodox iconography style. I had copied this look from the remake of the movie *Shaft*, in which Samuel L. Jackson's NYPD squad sport similar protective garments. I was told by the boss not to wear it, as it would offend non-Christians. Annoyed by his politically correct nonsense, I decided, in one of many impulsive moments, to join the river police.

Known as Thames Division colloquially, but actually called the Marine Policing Unit, this was traditionally a place where old cops went to see out their service, or for those cops obsessed with boats and sailing. In my naivety, I foolishly thought I could inject some youthful enthusiasm into this much-maligned area of policing. It was a uniformed role and definitely not something a detective went into.

I assumed it would be very cool, steaming up and down the river in fast boats, fighting crime and terrorism on the Thames and other London waterways. A good friend of mine already worked there and had encouraged me to apply. Frank, possibly the scruffiest fucker on the planet, had reliably informed me that the small unit he worked on was the crème de la crème of Thames Division and they had responsibility for a lot of plain-clothes proactive work on and around the river.

Buoyed by this (geddit?) I stuck in my application, much to the amusement of all my CID colleagues. All of them made substantial attempts to dissuade me from leaving, all except one of my bosses at the time, who made no effort to discourage me. It was no surprise that this was the same guy who had forbidden me to wear my famous 'Jesus' body armour.

The application procedure was surprisingly tough and involved a swimming test. The details I can't remember, but it involved several lengths of the pool at Hendon training school in a particular time frame. In full uniform. I mean, I was rather unfit, to say the least, and happily smoked 20 fags a day. Added to that, I hated swimming and was utterly shit at it. Still, I passed the test with about six seconds to spare.

After an interview, I was offered the job and gleefully took it. I think I enjoyed the fact that I was doing something totally untoward, career-wise. It was unexpected and unusual. It was typical that I would choose to do something slightly against the grain. CID colleagues scoffed when I turned up at the office having collected my river police uniform. I ignored them, eager to get on board the speeding police boats, clad in black dry suit with my Oakleys on, soaking up the London summer sun.

Well, it swiftly transpired that the vast majority of those at Thames Division, based at Wapping police station, were not the most proactive (or even active) of chaps and chapesses. The first few weeks, we were trained to drive the boats, which I found challenging, as I couldn't even drive a car at the time! We had training in tides, knots, rescues, sea survival, firefighting, intensive first aid and a lot more that I have since forgotten. It was fairly hardcore, I have to say. I soon understood, though, that this would be the most work I would actually do while on the unit.

After training, I managed to wangle a little time on the proactive team, which was excellent fun. Working with my trampy chum Frank and another guy I knew from Westminster, Jim, I spent a few weeks around Camden – it's got a lock, ergo it is part of the Thames Division remit – in uniform and in plain clothes nicking cannabis dealers and fighting (sometimes literally) criminals. It was like being back on a proper crime squad. We ended up with a commendation or two for our hard work. Jim, a former Royal Marine commando, was the hardest bloke I knew and he was always handy to have around. We would often be approached in plain clothes by drug dealers who would offer us gear. We would have to nick them there and then, as they had committed an offence, and, as per usual, they would fight us or try to escape as soon as we introduced ourselves. Jim was very adept at getting these guys on the floor. Most of them were big Gambian dudes. The looks on the faces of the custody staff were priceless when we dragged in a drug dealer, totally dishevelled and covered in mud and other riverbank detritus, especially as Thames Division officers were literally never seen in a custody suite, certainly not with a prisoner.

Those halcyon days quickly ended, though, and I was posted to my uniformed team. Working 12-hour shifts, we were responsible for first-line response to any river or water incidents. We had several fast boats and a van.

It was exactly like going back to the beginning, walking into Vine Street as a shiny new probationer. I strolled into the canteen at Wapping to meet my new colleagues. I had about seven years' service, I think, and in any other nick I would have been an experienced chap. Here, however, the next youngest in service on my new team had 21 years' experience. I was the bloody probby again!

Most of these guys had little or no street police experience; a lot of them had been on the boats for most of their service.

'Oooh, you won't be needing those,' scoffed one of the sergeants, nodding at my belt with the required weaponry attached to it.

'Well, you never know, sarge,' I said.

'You'll see,' he said. 'You're out on Marine Central with Paddy and Johnno.'

'OK,' I said, slightly apprehensive. I sat at a table with Paddy and Johnno, both of whom I had met during my boat training. They were leisurely tucking into a cooked breakfast. After two hours of hanging round, reading the papers and generally twiddling my thumbs, I eventually plucked up the courage to say to Paddy and Johnno, 'Are we gonna go out at any stage?'

Paddy yawned and stretched his arms.

'Yeah, c'mon, I suppose so,' he said. 'You can drive.' He chucked me the boat keys.

I hated driving the boats, absolutely hated it. I had no interest in them. I was more interested in policing the river – getting to know the criminals and having a nosy round some of the Eastern European vessels down at Barking.

Sullen, I led the way to the £250,000 250 Targa boat and, juddering, we pulled away. I tried to remember all the crap about tides and whatnot but failed and just pretended I was driving a dodgem or something. As we approached Southwark Bridge, I saw a massive tree-trunk in the water in front of us. This was fairly common and I knew it could cause damage to the boat if I hit it. Dutifully, I swerved to avoid it, but unfortunately I succeeded in moving us towards the lower part of the arch I had intended to pass through.

A combination of tide, poor steering and the boat's

broken reverse gear meant disaster was inevitable. Shoving me aside, Paddy tried desperately to get us away from the looming arch, but all to no avail.

CRAAAAASH!

To the unmistakable sounds of crunching, twisting metal, breaking glass and Johnno screaming, we ground to a halt, firmly wedged, it appeared.

I turned red with horror. If I'd had a full bladder, I would probably have pissed myself. I went to go on deck to see the damage, but Paddy grabbed me and, through clenched teeth, said, 'Just fucking stay inside.'

After some skilful piloting, and more grinding of steel and aluminium, Paddy managed to ease the boat out from under the bridge. I could see various bits of plastic and debris in the water around us.

I wished a hole would swallow me up. We chugged back to Wapping, an RNLI boat tooting its siren at us as it sped past. Paddy gave them the finger. 'They obviously fucking saw that,' he said.

Nothing was said to me en route back. As we neared Wapping, Johnno took the helm, and Paddy and I went on deck to check the damage. Oh dear. The entire antenna array and most of the pilot deck had been taken out. The boat was in a sorry state and looked horrendous. Apparently, it cost more than £20,000 to fix. Because it was Thames Division, everyone was incredibly laid-back about it and there were no repercussions for me. But in my view it was an omen and the death knell for my waterborne law-enforcement career. I never drove a police boat again.

The RNLI crew that buzzed past us after the 'incident' had apparently witnessed the whole thing and retrieved the blue light from the river. They dutifully brought it back to Wapping, where, unknown to me, it was mounted on a grand wooden plinth inscribed with my name!

The day after the crash, I agreed with my sergeant that Thames Division was not my bag, and I applied for a transfer. This took some weeks, however, and I spent a couple more months as a river cop, with the same team. I was downhearted, especially on night duties. Traditionally, the night was my favourite time to be a cop. Here, though, it was dire. Most of the crew would nip off and have a sleep. In the mornings, lots of night-duty officers would turn up for handover to the day shift with telltale bits of blue fluff on their uniform, from the Met Police blankets kept in the berths of the vessels for anyone picked out of the river.

So intense periods of complete boredom and depression interspersed with the odd dead body or call to a fight on a party boat became my work for a while. I used to wander up and down Wapping High Street during the day, desperate for a bit of action. It got so bad that the sergeant must have twigged. For my last three weeks as a river cop, I was sent out in plain clothes to Camden (although we spent a lot of time in Soho, a long way from any rivers) with another Thames Division officer to nick drug dealers and the like. It was always amusing to see the reaction of my partner for that day if we ended up in a custody suite with a prisoner. They would have no idea what was going on and would often admit that the last time they had dealt with a prisoner was way before I'd even joined the job.

I have to say, though, that, without exception, everyone I worked with at the river police was a genuinely good egg, despite the slightly different work ethic. Often, they would admit that they were not 'real cops' or that they had no interest in 'real policing'. Well, each to their own, I say. It wasn't my thing.

I had asked for a transfer to Camden – an area I had become quite familiar with while working on the river. However, that borough was, it seemed, full and the nearest vacancy was in Islington. I accepted the transfer, if only to get me out of the rut of river policing, and after six months my river career was over.

I worked at Islington in uniform for a few months, briefly enjoying the chases, the blue-light runs and the camaraderie of the team. But there was something missing and I was never very comfortable there. I yearned, I think, for the bright lights of central London, for the familiarity of crack whores and smackheads. I spent a lot of time at Islington around King's Cross. The area wasn't even in the borough, but I felt comfortable there; it reminded me of Soho, and indeed many of the same faces hung around there.

My penchant for moving around remained and I applied for the robbery squad at Islington. I had done similar work at West End Central and it would mean more regular hours – handy as Jane was pregnant again. I had to wait a while for the decision to be made, but I desperately needed to spice up my working days.

I hadn't had any TP work for a while, which I found rather mysterious. I was aware that other TP colleagues had been quite busy, so I called the SO10 administrator to make sure they had my contact details.

'Oh, hello, Christian,' she said. 'We thought you transferred to Avon and Somerset.'

This was indeed something I had considered but not followed up. Evidently there had been some wires crossed somewhere.

'Er, absolutely not. I'm still in the Met,' I said.

'OK. I'll let John know,' she replied.

Five minutes after I finished the call, my phone beeped. It was John.

'Hello, mate,' I said.

'Hello, young Christian,' he said. 'I've got a wee job in north-west London if you're available.'

'Thank Christ,' I thought. This would get me away from the boredom of everyday work.

'Yes, John. I am definitely available.'

7
BARBERSHOP

'WHA' THE FUCK YOU WAN'?'

In my head, a little voice, in very posh Queen's English, said, 'I'd like some crack cocaine, please!'

I looked quizzically at the 6-ft-5-in. Jamaican dude who had let me into the barbershop. And who had locked the door behind me.

I quickly took in my surroundings. A tiny 10-ft-square shop where there wasn't too much cutting going on. To be honest, I wouldn't have trusted any of these blokes with a crayon, let alone a pair of barbering shears. I noted the lack of actual barbers. No hair on the floor – just a haze of cannabis smoke and six or seven very big and intimidating Jamaican chaps.

My immediate worry was that I was locked in here. I clocked a nearby chair, which I thought I'd be able to chuck out the plate-glass window if I got in the shit. I also had my prop, a crutch, which I could brandish as a weapon if needed. I was acutely aware of my 'technical' – my body-worn recording equipment. Incredibly, this comprised a Sony Video Walkman connected to a tiny camera concealed about my person. The Walkman was the size of the latest John Grisham airport bestseller – in hardback – and had a big fat battery stuck on the end. How the Christ no one could see it, barely concealed under my clothes, I have no idea.

'Listen, bombaclaat, wha' you wan'?'

I was dressed down. Actually more 'down and out'. Unshaven, filthy and grimy, smelling of beer and urine, thanks to my colleagues, who had liberally doused my TP clothes with bodily fluids and the contents of a can of Stella. Bad tradecraft: it should have been Red Stripe for this job.

In any case, I thought, 'What the fuck do you think I want, idiot?', although my mouth, thankfully, said, 'Is there anything about? White?'

'Yeh, yeh, com, you cyan sit,' replied the big man.

I sat in an empty barber's chair. I took out £20 of the £30 I had been issued to buy the gear.

Big Man took about 20 rocks of crack out of his pocket.

'Just two, bruv,' I said. 'Bruv', a word I became intimately familiar with, was always the cops' way of sounding 'street'. I cringe now when I think about it, but it always seemed to work. Later on, it became 'blud', and in my last days of being 'down with the kids' a few years later I even graduated to using 'fam' – much to my teenage son's amusement.

Big Man grinned. A big toothy grin. Normal citizens would have seen this as friendly. I saw only something ominous. I was right.

'Where you from, white bwoy?'

'Er, round here.'

'Man, a nah see you before. You babylon?'

That meant 'police'.

'Nah, nah, bruv,' I stuttered. 'Course not.'

'Feh why you have a crutch?'

'Ah, mate, I hurt my leg, innit.' ('Innit' is another cop-cum-streetlife word – very antiquated and clichéd nowadays.)

Here I brandished my trump card, rolling up my trouser leg and displaying the *pièce de résistance* of my disguise: a filthy bandage around my calf, decorated with paint and make-up so that it looked as if a suppurating, weeping wound was hidden underneath.

Big Man crinkled his enormous face in disgust and motioned me to pull my trouser leg back down.

I did so and he appeared satisfied, handing me two of the rocks of crack from his palm. I handed over my 20 quid and, keen to get out of there, I jumped up, feeling a strange tug and a click in the small of my back as I did so.

Hmmmm. The small of my back (appropriately named, as it wasn't big enough!) was where my ridiculously large video Walkman was 'concealed'. I knew the strange tug I'd felt was the lead feeding the camera to the Walkman coming out. Unbeknown to me, it was now dangling, visible, between my legs like a tail.

Big Man unbolted the door to the barbershop and I hobbled out, happy and relieved to have broken the ice with our targets. I gingerly put the two rocks of crack in the coin pocket of my jeans and walked, in an ungainly manner, back to my car. En route, horrified, I realised that the wire had come completely loose and was quite noticeable. I grabbed the lead and unceremoniously stuffed it into the waistband of my jeans. I could sort that out later.

Panic started to course through me. Did this mean I hadn't recorded the all-important deal? Worse still, did it mean that the barbershop posse had seen the wire as I left? If that were the case, then my next visit would not be so friendly.

When I got back to the derelict police station we were using as a base, I hurriedly stripped myself of the encumbering Walkman, nervously rewound the tape and pressed play. I said a silent prayer to the police gods. Come on. Please have caught something. The little flip-out screen on the Walkman clicked into life. There was Big Man approaching me. There was the nervous exchange. Then – bingo! – there was the buy. The wire must have come loose only when I stood up. At least the relevant evidence was captured.

If the only evidence we needed had been one buy, it would have been job done. Sadly, it rarely works that way. Now we'd had a bit of success, we needed to get more evidence on tape. It meant I'd have to go back in there again. I'd been lucky once, but if Big Man or any of his posse had caught sight of my dangling wire, I would be for it the next time I showed my face in there.

A day or so later, it was time for another buy. I spent the entire preparation in a state of fear, remembering that sinking feeling when I knew I might have been compromised. My nerves were jangling. That might just have worked in my favour, though, as now I didn't need any acting skills to accurately portray the jittering junkie.

Using the crutch as a prop again, I made my way to the barbershop once more. This time, there seemed to be more of the posse hanging around, all of them glaring at me menacingly as I entered.

I dispensed with the small talk. 'Two,' I muttered, holding up two stinking fingers.

There was a pause. The assembled crew looked at Big

Man to see how he'd respond. This is when I'd find out how observant he'd been when I left last time.

The fear started to build, but just when I thought it was going to turn very nasty very quickly, he stepped off his chair, approached me and revealed two rocks in his clammy palm.

Another deal in the bag.

For the next couple of weeks, I went back in the same guise, and every time I was successful. Before long, though, I had to ditch my crutch. The complaint was that I took too long to walk to the plot, thanks to my exaggerated leg injury. I could scarcely believe it. Time-consuming it might be, but it was producing results. The DI running the job was unequivocal about it, though, and ordered me to lose the crutch, which, sadly, I did.

The crutch had done the trick, though. By that time, I was a well-known face at the barber's and had no problem gathering further evidence to help our case. After about three months of activity, the arrest phase finally took place. The premises were raided and all of our subjects were arrested. The barber's and other related places got searched, and to my surprise the team retrieved, amongst other things, a gun.

Only then did it hit home to me the type of characters I'd been dealing with. If they'd been genuinely suspicious that I was police, I could have been done for. These guys, although only serving up £10 and £20 deals, obviously had access to guns. I got the impression that, had they suspected anything, they would have had no qualms about showing off their gangsta credentials. It was a good result all round, but also a lesson for me to always be ultra wary.

When the suspects were shown the video footage of

me going in the barber's and around the area doing deals with them, they all stated that they were giving me change, that I was begging for cash and I was a local drunk. I'm told that when they were let in on the fact that I was a cop, they were incredulous and unbelieving – priceless looks on their faces, apparently!

Just when I was beginning to relax, the job had a final sting in the tail. Some weeks later, I received a call from John, the TP coordinator. He had arranged for a chap from the Met's Technical Support Unit to come and install a personal attack alarm at my home. I was baffled. 'Why?' I asked. Apparently, some of the suspects had obtained a still photograph of me and another TP from the job (presumably it had been mistakenly disclosed to the defence) and had clubbed together to slap a £5,000 bounty on my head. I thought this was a slight overreaction on their part; after all, it was only a couple of hundred quid's worth of street drugs they had sold me. But the information came from a very reliable informant and the threat was being taken seriously. Armed with that information, I consented to the alarm, but I'd rather have been armed with a gun to protect the family and myself. That would have been a better idea.

It was also slightly disconcerting to realise your life was valued at only five grand. I thought I was worth way more than that!

So, after my second TP job, I had an alarm installed in my house and was a marked man with a contract out on my life. Welcome to the covert world.

The success of that job meant, however, that I was too busy to sit around worrying about hit men knocking at my door. In the weeks and months after that, there wasn't a time when I wasn't engaged on a TP operation on top of my day job. I was working flat-out, doing 60–70 hour weeks.

But, after the stresses of the barbershop job, John obviously thought I deserved something a bit more refined as a reward. I soon found myself with three other TPOs in a very swish central London nightclub. We had been issued with hundreds of quid each. We were to go in and slip the bouncers £20 each to get into the VIP area. We were to then swan about sipping champagne cocktails and trying to score cocaine from likely suspects. It was as far removed from a Jamaican barber's as you could get.

Needless to say, we attacked our task with enthusiasm. No piss-soaked jeans for this job – just pissed-up coppers! One evening in particular, one of the other TPOs (a lady called Maria) went slightly overboard with the champagne and we had to abort the job after only a couple of hours in the club. She was absolutely hammered, to the extent that she had difficulty keeping her head up and her eyes open. It was like a scene from one of those 'broken Britain' type programmes about binge drinking. We desperately tried to sober her up before going back to the nick, by literally pouring black coffee down her throat. It was to no avail, however, and we sheepishly sat in the nick trying to write our evidential notes as she drunkenly lolled around, the untidy scrawl in her notebook completely illegible. I think after that episode she went on a forced 'sabbatical' from TP work for a while.

I did a few more TP jobs in Haringey and Hackney. These were a far cry from my first job, where all the stops had been pulled out. They were done on a tight budget.

Often, these operations revolved solely around 'cold calling'. My worst nightmare. I mean, I hate calling anyone on the phone. I'd rather email or text. I would be a shit telesales person. Sometimes, incredibly, it worked. Mostly, though, the dealers would either say, 'Fuck off,' or claim they had no idea what I was on about and put the phone down.

We would always call them back, sometimes to the point of them getting very irate on the phone. Occasionally, they would call back and ask for 'DC Smith from Tottenham police station' or something similar, so they knew the tactic we were using.

When the calls were successful, we would have to meet these idiots. We had no idea who they were, what their history was, what they looked like, whether they were nasty bastards or not. It was doing these jobs that helped refine my 'magic eye'. Eventually, I could tell in a split second who the dealer was as they approached to meet me, even though I had never met them before.

There would always be that little modicum of suspicion. A first-time meeting was like an awkward blind date. Both of us wanted to get the first deal over and done with, me because I didn't know who I was dealing with and thought they might think I was a cop, and them because they thought I might be a cop. These initial deals were always hurried, but the second and third times were usually easier. It would end up getting to be a comfortable relationship and you'd find yourself discussing nice subjects with some of these crack dealers – families, Christmas, holidays. It was actually like going to the hairdresser's.

Once, on the day of an arrest phase for an operation in Haringey, I had met up with one guy and he had served me up my usual £20 of crack. He was a nice chap. Very articulate and lived with his little old mum.

'Chris, you know I like you, yeah?'

'Yeah, of course,' I answered nervously

'Well, will you tell me one thing?' he said.

God almighty. 'What now?' I thought. 'Does he want a date? Does he want to know where I got my fake earring from?'

'Yep,' I said.

'Are you a police officer?'

My heart jumped and I looked quizzically at him.

'Why do you ask?' I said. 'It's a fucking ridiculous question, you dick.'

'Oh, just because, you know, if you were a police officer, you would have to say yes. Undercover police can't lie if they're asked straight out, you see.'

I too had heard this bullshit urban myth. 'Oh,' I said 'I dunno about that.'

We parted seconds later, and the last I saw of him was two burly Haringey cops grabbing him up and nicking him. Poor guy with his misguided idea.

Other times, we would assist the counties with TP jobs. This was generally seen as the physical equivalent of cold calling. We'd get thrown into a strange town and told to wander around and buy as many drugs as possible. From Sussex to South Wales, I worked in all sorts of towns, villages and estates.

Occasionally, I would get another plum nightclub job, seemingly as a reward for putting in my time on the mean streets.

As my tally of operations grew considerably, my headaches started to get more intense and more frequent. I just put these down to the stresses and strains of being busy, doing TP jobs left, right and centre as well as my day job.

I loved being busy – to the detriment of my home life,

my kids. At work, I could happily worry about and deal with other people's problems, other people's crimes or mistakes; I didn't have to think about mine.

But then, what did I have to be stressed about? I was doing the job I loved.

8

IN THE CRACK HOUSE

IF I'D THOUGHT INFILTRATING THE BARBERSHOP WAS A tricky assignment, it was nothing compared with my next one.

This time, they wanted me to get inside a real crack house. This type of establishment is more or less what it says on the tin: a place where crack and heroin are bought, sold and consumed. Often, the genuine tenant has been forced to allow the drug dealers in. Threats of violence are common. Or the tenant is a crackhead or smackhead and the promise of free gear in exchange for the use of their flat or house is just far too tempting an offer to turn down.

In a quiet residential street in Richmond, sandwiched between two similar Victorian houses, was our target. It looked fairly normal. Certainly the other properties in the street were typical middle-class London, all John Lewis blinds and Farrow & Ball-painted doors. This one lacked a certain *je ne sais quoi* and its true nature was revealed by the frequent comings and goings of various ne'er-do-wells. The local Neighbourhood Watch coordinator had complained to the police.

It didn't take the world's greatest detective to ascertain

exactly what was going on here. Black men from Jamaica (a rarity in this particular street) had set up shop in the house, encouraging pasty-faced heroin users and hardcore crack whores to turn up at all hours to purchase their wares. Evidently, they had no worries about disturbing the environment; I mean, you couldn't have set up shop in a less appropriate place!

It hadn't taken long for the neighbours to alert the police, but the reality of modern policing meant these residents were lucky action was being taken. Each borough might have had a small team of officers, but drug squads were not widespread in the Met during this time. The simple truth was that drugs were not deemed a priority.

It was very easy for senior management of boroughs to say they didn't have a drug problem. The only way you would find drug crimes being reported was if the police found out about them. If you don't find drug crimes, you don't have a drug problem. My belief was that if you handled the problem you'd make people's lives easier. I always thought how awful it was for the neighbours who found themselves living in the shadow of a crack den. I felt for the little old ladies who lived above one of these squalid flats or who had to walk past a line of craven junkies every day. That's awful.

Sadly, the resources weren't always there to help these people. Sometimes, though, you could circumvent the system. Money was often made available to boroughs to accommodate overtime for a particular operation. In order to get this injection of cash, you had to find a way of linking the operation to the borough's priorities. In other words, to tackle a drug problem, you always had to link it to acquisitive crime, like burglaries. In order for us to smash this crack house, it wasn't enough that we knew dozens of criminals frequented it every day. We had to show that by stopping the operation we'd be reducing burglaries and street crime in the area. That usually proved quite easy to do. In this case, the borough commanders could confidently say that if the crack house was taken out, house break-ins nearby would be reduced, thereby making residents feel safer in their homes. It was all waffle and spurious links, really, but an opportunity was found.

Another factor to take into consideration was that there was always kudos to be had from running a covert op. Test purchasing looked good: you got good evidence, you got good crime figures and a positive result meant praise for the officers involved. Everyone's happy.

It was just down to people like me to make the whole thing happen. Despite the fact that we were in a delightful part of London, the idea of going into a real crack den was still somewhat unnerving for me. A very experienced TP, Victor, who looked like an anorexic 6-ft-7-in. tramp (think Louis Theroux with longer hair and an eating disorder), had already been in the house once.

At the initial briefing, Victor told how the doors were bolted and there was always a well-built chap guarding the door. The back door was welded shut, so there was only one way out, unless you jumped out of the front windows.

Nervously, I 'kitted up' with a body-worn camera and a monitoring device that allowed the operational team to hear what was going on. A vanload of beefy riot cops were going to be round the corner to smash things up if we needed a rescue.

Victor drove us to the crack house in a battered Ford Escort. I mentally prepared myself to go into the unknown. I was going to be doing something that many cops never had the chance to (and indeed might have preferred not to): seeing life behind the locked doors of a crack house.

The street was deathly quiet when Victor banged on the door. It was opened by a black guy in his 30s, dressed all in dark clothes with a black baseball cap. He nodded in recognition at Victor, and we were in.

Following Victor, I stepped into the darkened hallway. I felt a bit like a new boy at school or a Spurs fan in the home stand at Stamford Bridge: totally fucking uncomfortable and extremely ill at ease. I knew that my usual TP get-up of filthy clothes, big furry hooded parka and battered packet of fags, as well as my clinically applied make-up, would only go so far now I was truly on the other side of the fence. Behind me, the doorman slid shut three solid bolts. I didn't have time to assess my surroundings. Victor led me into the front room. Although it was the middle of the afternoon, the room was shrouded in darkness. Tatty, dark blankets covered the windows. It stank. Of crack, of fags and of that unusual odour of dirty human beings. And it was filled with a throng of people. I was faced with a scene of utter human devastation. Maybe about 30 people in all, a wide variety of ages and races, were sitting around the room. This was the kind of life that few ever get to see, aside from in those impressive *Panorama* documentaries or the best gritty French *policiers*. You really had to be there to comprehend the sights and especially the smells, to appreciate what a complete state the place was. It was heaving. Yet, for the number of people, there was little hubbub, just quiet conversations amongst those who evidently already knew one another. Everyone was united by one common purpose: to score.

I knew that if any one of these desperate drug users had had any inkling as to who we were, we would have been summarily beaten, at best. I was sure that every single person in the house would have been on the receiving end of police attention at some recent time. Their lives and mine couldn't have been more different. Yet here we were, together.

We found a space on the floor to sit down and, eavesdropping, I was astounded to hear that every conversation was about heroin or crack. No one was discussing anything else. The main subject appeared to be when the gear would arrive. 'Great,' I thought. We had to wait for the fucking dealer. Victor had warned me that this might be the case.

We were viewed with a little suspicion. Some of the more loquacious of the assembled junkies questioned us. Who were we, how did we know about the place, who did we know? It sounded interrogatory, but in fact it was what passed for junkie small talk, trying to establish who our acquaintances were. I was fearful of slipping up or saying the wrong thing. My worst fear was being recognised as a cop by some crackhead from Soho who had decided to move west. It was entirely possible. Soho drug users were the most nomadic around. In the dank half-light, however, it was quite difficult to make out people's faces clearly.

As a uniform cop, you think these junkies are scum and shit. They often take the blame for their lot, but I felt a lot of pity for them. I would have liked to talk to them about football or travel or their plans for life, or something else inane or inconsequential, but all they wanted to talk about was drugs. That was it. No one talked about their families or their work or their weekend. Just gear.

With no idea of how long the dealer might take to arrive, we had no option but to sit it out. Given how many people were hanging around expectantly, I assumed it wouldn't be long before he showed up. I was wrong. The minutes dragged into hours. It was intolerable. The air was thick with fag smoke and the odd stench you only find with drug addicts. At one stage, I started to wonder if I would ever see daylight again. The longer I was in there, the more my anxiety grew. I realised that the recording device was going to run out by the time it was needed. It only lasted two hours. Three hours after we'd first entered the house, we were still sitting there talking about drugs, trying to remember our flimsy cover stories, which were designed to withstand only the most casual scrutiny.

I was mentally exhausted from adopting the ridiculous faux-street accent I used to use. Thankfully, crackheads aren't the greatest conversationalists, but even the pressure of keeping exchanges going with the odd 'bruv' here and there was tiring.

Eventually, after an eternity, the dealer appeared. He was a light-skinned black guy called Francis and one of his accompanying minions started dishing out the gear. Victor and I swiftly made our purchases – a tenner each for a rock – and left. In terms of evidence, we had nothing. Our only consolation was that we'd successfully infiltrated the house and managed to sweat it out without being challenged. The path was clear for us to return another day.

Over the next few weeks, we went back several more times. The set-up was nearly always the same: dozens of desperadoes hanging around awaiting their fix. The only aspect that altered was the length of time Francis took to arrive.

Soon, the operational team decided it was time to close the crack house down. They had identified the main players but wanted to raid the place in the midst of a deal, which meant Victor and I would need to be inside when the bust went down.

It was very exciting being at the final briefing, knowing that the dealers were going to be taken out and the crack den closed for good. And I would be smack bang in the middle of it! The DI outlined the plan to the 40 assembled officers. They were mainly riot cops and local drug-squad officers. Some of the riot cops would be wearing special 'glass suits' that would allow them to clamber through the front and back windows of the house unimpeded and free from injury once they had smashed the shit out of them. Essentially, the house would get absolutely trashed, for maximum distraction impact, and it was anticipated that the officers would have the entire place secured in seconds.

I was more than happy with this. My adrenalin was pumping. I had no portent of any impending headache as I usually did. Certainly after all the previous deployments into this house, my headaches had been extremely intense. The absence of a painful bonce was probably because the operational team had thought of everything. The toilet was blocked so no one could flush any drugs away.

When we arrived at the house, I went into the lounge, where this time Francis was waiting. Victor had already bought his gear and I gave Francis £20 for two rocks. He opened up a battered Benson & Hedges box, which I could see was stuffed to the gunnels with rocks of crack. He was just about to pick out two near the top when: BANG! BANG! CRASH!

The windows were going in. At the same time, the door, despite its bolts, was getting smashed to smithereens. The boys were coming in.

Panicked, Francis didn't know what to do. His eyes were

wide with fear and worry. Gone was the nonchalance of the local crack baron; instead, I saw a frightened young boy, probably wishing he had stayed in Jamaica.

Instinctively, I screamed at him, 'Give me the fucking gear, bruv.' He looked at me, stunned. 'I'll flush it down the bog.'

Incredibly, he handed me the fag packet stuffed with gear. I ran into the hallway, where all hell was breaking loose. It was like being caught in a tornado. The noise was phenomenal. All I could hear was smashing glass, splintering wood and screams of 'Police! Police!'

I'd never experienced anything like it. I didn't get too far in the hallway, as by that time the front door had been breached and the big doorman was on the floor, literally being trampled on by cops. One of them steamed into me, pushing me face first against the wall. The cuffs were on me in seconds.

Then, incredibly, just as quickly as it had begun, all was calm again. The house was a fucking mess. There was wood and glass everywhere. I was pushed into the lounge, where I saw Francis and the doorman along with Victor and a few others. All were sporting handcuffs.

In my head, I was grinning. In fact, I was beaming furiously. Victor did a bit of play-acting for the benefit of Francis and his cronies, calling the cops 'cunts' and whatnot. He and I were led out first into a waiting drug-squad car. We were pleased. We knew we had closed the crack house, got several dealers arrested and recovered a significant amount of crack (it turned out to be 76 rocks). A minuscule seizure by SO10 standards, granted, but a nice result nonetheless.

As we were led out, a small gathering of neighbours watched from across the road. They were looking disdainfully at us. I could see the utter contempt in their eyes. They all looked as if they could spit on us. Certainly none of them looked at us with pity or sadness. We represented the bane of their lives in the neighbourhood. We were complete scumbags as far as they were concerned. They saw two sad, useless, stinking junkies getting nicked, that was all.

If only they'd known.

9

OPERATION SCARECROW

ALTHOUGH THE DRIZZLE WAS LIGHT, MY 'SHOWERPROOF' mac was soaked through, and the suit and tie stuck to me with all the comfort of a straitjacket. I was never one for smart clothes at the best of times, but here, in the dark and wet, I felt a right pillock. Still, I kept telling myself, it was a bank holiday and I was on double time. There were always worse ways to earn a crust than walking around in the rain.

The mobile-phone earpiece I was wearing crackled with static. I could barely hear the intermittent instructions, but I just made out the detective sergeant who was running the operation telling me to slow down a bit. I adjusted the laptop bag on my shoulder. It was supposed to look as though it was carrying the latest gear. In actual fact, it was filled with photocopier paper. Did they have to pack so much into it, though? It was bloody heavy. The brand-spanking-new mobile phone in my right hand was purposely lit up like a Christmas tree. As if that wasn't enticing enough, I staggered slightly drunkenly as I walked.

Hopefully, I looked the perfect target for a robbery. That was the plan, anyway.

This was a TP job with a difference: playing the decoy.

A gang of violent robbers had been carrying out a spate of particularly nasty raids on men returning from work via Greenwich station to a well-to-do new-build waterfront housing complex. Combating robberies was a big issue for the Met, which had launched Operation Scarecrow in response to these attacks.

I was one of three officers taking it turns to walk the route in an attempt to flush out the gang. It all sounds rather exciting, but the reality was that these jobs were more often than not uneventful. It was rare, if not unheard of, for a decoy officer to actually get robbed. With this in mind, I was totally at ease, happy to spend 20 minutes in the early hours of the morning wandering around the prescribed route. This was my third night at it and so far we hadn't seen anything suspicious. Tonight, though, we were keeping it going until a bit later, as the night before a man and his girlfriend had been the victims of a vicious assault just half an hour after we had called it a day. She had been held on the ground, her life threatened, until her man handed over his cards, complete with pin numbers.

That's why, at 2.30 a.m., I was giving it one last circuit. Despite the fact that the gang's most recent attack had taken place in the middle of our operation, I still believed that the chances of us encountering them were less than slim. In this weather, even the destitute would be seeking cover. The only people out and about were the last stragglers from the pub and the odd group of youths larking about.

My earpiece crackled once more. 'Stop by the river and make a call.'

I duly did. Slightly over-egging my part, I whipped out my very desirable smartphone and, with the rain still failing, made a show of drunkenly swaying as I slurred my words, 'speaking' on the phone to no one in particular. After about ten minutes, I decided it was time to go back to the safety of the unmarked pick-up car round the corner. I happily hoisted the laptop bag further up my shoulder and began to meander back.

'Chris, wait there, mate. Just wait there.' The DS was back in my earpiece.

Feeling slightly perturbed, I did so, maintaining my vaguely drunken guise. I looked out across the filthy Thames and didn't really register what he said next.

'Right. There's five black guys behind you. They are looking you up and down. They might do you.'

I heard footsteps behind me, then realised they were running. I couldn't help but turn around.

'Fuck me, they're robbing the decoy! Go, go, go!' screamed the DS in my ear.

Right at that moment, I saw several black faces almost on top of me. The face of one of the robbers in particular, creased with anger and venom, will be etched on my mind forever. In a flash, they were all over me. I was pushed, grabbed, pulled and spun around as the laptop bag was wrenched from my shoulder. The phone I was holding fell to the ground.

My so-called valuables gone, I cowered, expecting them to grab their haul and move on. 'Just leave me alone,' I said.

They weren't done with me yet, though. In milliseconds, I was dragged up, hauled one way and then pushed against the railings, below which was the dark water of the Thames. I felt sure this was the gang we wanted. They had threatened to chuck their victims in the river before.

Smack! Smack! I was punched twice in the face as I felt hands going into my pockets. The black lads had surrounded me. 'This is it,' I thought. 'I'm going in the fucking river.'

Bizarrely, in a split second of clarity, I began to plan for a plunge into the icy depths. I remembered my survival training from the river police. I knew I would be consumed by the shock of hitting the icy black water immediately. If I prepared myself mentally for that, it might not affect me so badly. As long as I understood this and was ready to swim a bit, I should be fine. I would only have a couple of minutes before hypothermia would begin to set in. Then I'd be in deep shit.

But, just as I braced myself to be tipped over the railings, my assailants' grip loosened and, as quickly as it had begun, my ordeal finished. The gang was scarpering. I heard dogs barking, shouts of 'Stop! Police!' I knew that the arrest team, with two police dogs, who had been cooped up in an office only yards away for about six hours, had been released and were chasing down the perpetrators.

Leaning against the railing, breathing heavily, I tried to compose myself. I saw that one of the robbers had been detained only about 20 yards away and had fallen to his knees. He kept trying to get up. A plain-clothes officer was striking him with his baton, screaming, 'Get on the fucking floor! Get on the fucking floor!' Each baton strike was timed to coincide with each fervent command to lie down.

I sat shakily on the soaked pavement. I felt utterly fucked. Jittering with adrenalin, I felt the rain saturate my trousers as my head spun.

'C'mon, mate,' said one of the DCs on the arrest team, grabbing my arm and hauling me to my feet. 'You OK?' he asked.

'Er, I think so,' I replied, not really knowing what had gone on, to be honest. Bundled into a waiting unmarked car, I was sped to the local police station.

In the car, as the city lights flashed by, I thought I was

pulling myself together. The reality of what had happened started to sink in.

'Wow,' I thought. 'We got them. We actually bloody got them.' No doubt I was still in shock; the terror I'd felt only moments earlier was replaced by pure adrenalin. I got robbed! The operation fucking worked. I could scarcely believe it. What a massive high!

As I strode into the local CID office, where the DS and DI were waiting, my broad smile couldn't convey the extent of the elation I was feeling. I gladly accepted praise from them. With the typical bravado of a cop, I was now ready to brush the incident off as all part of the service, as the whole episode was gleefully recounted to me from their perspective.

I soon learned that four of the five robbers had been nicked. Three of those four had had to go to hospital for nasty dog bites and other injuries received as they attempted to escape. One of them had even tried to flee along the riverbank but must have got the shock of his life when he was huckled by the river police, clad in black wetsuits and balaclavas to look especially intimidating. (He subsequently filed a formal complaint stating that he had been 'assaulted by a commando'!)

The DS and DI were overjoyed at the success of the operation and, as the rest of the team made their way back into the office, the praise continued to be heaped upon me. An old PC, one of the dog handlers, who had obviously seen it all and done it all, patted me between the shoulder blades and said, 'Well done, mate. Well done. You've got some bollocks, I tell you.' That meant the world to me.

I was still buzzing from the great result as I wrote my statement on the incident. Then the shock wore off and the enormity of what happened – and, more importantly, what could have happened – hit me. I realised I'd just experienced one of the scariest moments of my life. I'd genuinely believed I might be going to die. I relived the moment when I thought I was taking a nosedive over those railings. Panic coursed through me once again. Even though I'd known there was a river police RIB (Rigid Inflatable Boat) patrolling the water, for a split second I'd felt sure the icy cold of Old Father Thames was going to do me in.

My lip started trembling. I felt tears well up. Somehow, though, I gulped them down and maintained a brave face for the delighted throng of officers who had put so much work into catching these little shits. I couldn't let them see weakness in my eyes now. I completed the paperwork and, with the congratulatory comments ringing in my ears, clocked off for the night.

I don't think I had any idea of the effect the incident had had on me until the next day.

'You OK, Christian?' asked my sergeant as I reported for my normal day job at Islington. 'You're quiet today. Not your usual self.'

'Actually, sarge, I did a robbery decoy job last night and got robbed.'

'Oooh, well done! Double time too, eh?' (It's funny how police focus on that part.)

'Er, yes. I was wondering, though, can I just fuck off home, please? I'm not feeling too good, actually.'

She looked a bit surprised. 'Of course, mate.'

I ran to the toilets and vomited. Then, without telling anyone else, I went home. Walking the streets, I found myself avoiding groups of youths on the Tube and in the street.

The robbers all received hefty prison terms. It transpired

that just hours before I was attacked they'd robbed another man and smashed him around the head with a hammer. They'd left the weapon in a stolen car parked round the corner from where they'd assaulted me. When I heard this detail, it only served to shake me up even further. When I thought how close I'd come to a severe injury – perhaps leaving lasting damage – it messed me up even more. These thugs were serious criminals, clearly getting a buzz from the violence they inflicted on their innocent victims.

The incident affected my day job. At the time, I was working out of Islington, for CID, dealing with robberies. These cases were much smaller beer than the gang in Greenwich. I did think it somewhat ironic, however, that a copper working on robberies ended up getting robbed himself. But what happened did help to give me some empathy with the victims I came into contact with in Islington. I could sympathise with them more and, after that, whenever I went to speak to someone who had been robbed I did a lot more than I normally would for them.

These robberies really were petty, however. We called them 'schoolboy robberies' because literally it would be one badly brought up schoolboy stealing from another and then someone would phone the police. It was pretty dispiriting and a complete contrast to the type of work I was doing with the test purchasing.

On occasion on the robbery squad we would help out with burglaries. I remember coming in one morning and there were two prisoners who had been arrested for nicking things from a building site. They were both young lads from Islington. I read through the circumstances and I saw they were pissed and they'd just been mucking about. I interviewed the boys and went up to speak to the families. I told them this was a load of rubbish. It was hardly the crime of the century and they seemed pretty contrite once they'd sobered up and could see the consequences of their actions.

I thought I'd deal with it accordingly and let them off with a warning. However, I was told that, because burglary figures were high and we had to show that people were not only being caught but also prosecuted to the full extent of the law, I had to charge them with burglary. I'm all for criminals being punished, but on this occasion I didn't agree. It wasn't what I'd joined the police for. It wasn't something I could say no to, though. The Crown Prosecution Service agreed with the decision and they went ahead and pressed charges. It should be noted, however, that the CPS is under the same scrutiny in relation to figures and results as the police.

I was so disillusioned I let the paperwork slide on purpose, but I still ended up in court nine months later when the case was called at Snaresbrook Crown Court. The two boys turned up and they were in tears. This wasn't your usual tale of bad boys running riot. They were accompanied by their families. As I watched them trying to come to terms with the situation, I thought, 'How have I allowed this to happen?' I decided to have a word with the prosecutor and persuaded her that the charges were a load of nonsense and the case shouldn't have got this far. She wasn't happy with this because it meant she had to stand up in front of the judge and explain why the case was being dropped. The only good thing was that she had only begun working on the case quite recently and was able to say with some conviction that it was a mistake that it had got so far.

I had managed to get the case thrown out and the families were so grateful they invited me to a free meal at a restaurant one of the parents owned. I never took them up on the offer. The outcome didn't affect the police in the slightest. They had got their crime solved and their figures down the minute the lads had been charged. As far as the police are concerned, what happens after that is nothing to do with them.

That Operation Scarecrow continued to have a negative effect on me. Even months after the incident, I was wary of groups of youths, specifically black youths, and would not get into any sort of confrontation with any suspects at work. Even now, years and years later, I will nervously scan my environment, looking for any huddled groups of youngsters or anyone I think looks like they want to rob me. It has been an awful way to live, but it's part of who I am now.

On every subsequent test purchase course, I would give a presentation about the operation, about how I felt and how it affected me. I always found these presentations really quite cathartic, although it was difficult to stem the tide of emotion that was aching to come out.

I have still never quite got over it. I know it was a police operation, I was never really in too much danger, there were loads of cops hidden nearby to save me – but that doesn't take away the impact of the incident at all.

It was my first experience of a serious assault, but I felt that if I admitted it had messed me up it could affect my chances of getting on for the rest of my career. Potentially, I wanted to become an undercover officer, so I didn't make any waves about it. I didn't say to anyone that I wanted to see Occupational Health for some counselling or that I had any issues at all.

I was offered counselling, but, as I believed was expected, I declined. I felt sure that had I accepted, I wouldn't have been going out on any more covert operations. I was convinced that my card would have been marked, that I'd have been considered some sort of stressed-out wuss. The last thing I wanted was that sort of stigma. The best way to deal with it (or so I thought at the time) was to work harder and longer.

'Bring it on,' I thought.

10

THE WORLD'S GREATEST CON MAN

'CHRISTIAN, YOU ARE JUST SUCH A FUCKING NOMAD. Never happy, are you?' joked my DS at Islington.

'But, sarge, I really wanna go. It would be great for me,' I said.

'OK, OK,' she said, smiling.

I had been offered a job back in central London on the Hotel Crime Unit. Sadly, it no longer exists, but at the time it was run by Andy, a DS with whom I shared an affinity for catching villains and grafting very hard. Andy, in fact, was blessed with the world's most incredible luck, especially when it came to police work. And gambling. Confident and self-assured, he was a good leader and came to be a good friend.

I had to have a formal interview, with Andy and Seamus, another DS I knew. I had swotted up on all the relevant legislation, but, when it came down to it, they hit me with such a barrage of bizarre questions, about hotel policies and how I could blag free hotel rooms, that I wondered if this was the move for me after all. Andy looked at me and said, 'OK, last question, mate. Can you tell me five hotels in central London that begin with the letter "H"?'

'Er, Hilton,' I stammered, ' . . . er . . .' I looked pleadingly at Andy.

I saw the slightest smile on his lips and said, 'Are you joking, Andy?'

'Course I am, you dick,' he said. 'You've got the job. You start Monday.'

And so I was introduced to the heady world of luxurious (and sometimes not so luxurious) West End hotels, investigating professional criminals, thieving staff, bag snatchers, pickpockets and fraudsters, along with hard to crack cases beyond the capability and resources of local CID officers.

Andy and I were allowed substantial free rein to undertake whatever work we wanted. We maintained a fairly impressive reputation amongst the custody suites and CPS lawyers in central London, often helped by my introduction that we were from 'Scotland Yard's Hotel Crime Unit', when really we were nothing but a couple of hardworking cops based at Charing Cross nick.

We dealt with some fascinating jobs and we worked hard. I was still doing test purchase work on top of this day job and was often turned away from some of the nicer hotels mid-investigation because of my long hair and unshaven phizog.

I still tried to specialise in drug offences and kept up a good working knowledge of street drugs. Andy and I would often, if bored, wander around Soho and the West End nicking people for drug offences, despite them having nothing to do with hotels. We were cops, first and foremost, and that was what we did. I loved it. It was almost as good as the crime squad days in Soho.

THE WORLD'S GREATEST CON MAN

When a hotel guest from Holland left 25,000 ecstasy tablets in his hotel room in Park Lane, I jumped onto the investigation immediately. The Dutch guy was obviously not blessed with the greatest criminal mind, as he had checked in using his real name and real ID. It didn't take long to arrange his arrest with colleagues in Holland, and, armed with the ecstasy, along with a licence from the Home Office to export Class A drugs, I met up with a detective counterpart in Amsterdam, who took me through the evidence they had accrued on my suspect. They had arrested him (using a SWAT team) in his back garden as he was building a bomb, which he intended to use to assassinate an Albanian crime lord in Italy. The Dutch gratefully prosecuted him for the drugs. This was just one of many jobs we had with an international bent.

We would look for linked series, crimes with a similar method, MO or suspects. One series of burglaries had us stumped for months. Several hotels in the Holiday Inn, Premier Inn and Travelodge chains reported a spate of break-ins. It appeared the thieves were somehow breaking into bedrooms, stealing valuables and making their escape, leaving no trace behind them. It was remarkable. There were no obvious signs of a break-in, nothing was disturbed in the rooms and there were no suspicious sightings for us to go on. At first, we believed it was a sophisticated inside job.

Then we discovered how they were managing to get into the rooms undetected. They would drill a tiny 3-mm hole into the door, next to the lock, using an old hand drill. They would then insert thin filament wire with a loop on the end through the hole, snag the loop on the handle, pull it down and open the door.

That was ingenious. But what made the thieves extra

special was that once they'd been inside the room and taken what they wanted they would fill the hole inside and out with putty exactly the same colour as the door. It was so professional. After that we dubbed the thieves 'the Door Drillers'.

Then, almost by chance, someone at one of the affected hotels clocked a car that might have been used in the robberies. It was a blue BMW. We had the registration and it belonged to a lady in Hampstead, who was clearly innocent. She had evidently had her number plate nicked and cloned. At the time, the City of London's ring of steel was the only area where automatic cameras could pick up car registrations. We put in the details of the BMW on the off-chance that the Door Drillers drove through there.

In the meantime, we were chasing leads all over the South-east and had reports of similar raids further afield, all over the country. We discovered they'd done 50 rooms in each hotel. You had to really look for the holes. We were finding doors all over the place. Eventually, we had images of them on CCTV but no names.

Then, lo and behold, the car got stopped in the City and two men were arrested. One was a fat bloke who had nothing to do with the robberies. The other chap I'll call Pyotr Slavovic. He was a proper criminal, one of the few I got to meet. We searched the BMW and it had all the tools of the trade. We found the putty there. We had the samples from each door, so we had them analysed and matched them to what was in the car.

He hadn't come to the attention of the police before. We tried to get checks done in Serbia, to no avail. Nevertheless, we had enough to charge him with several of the robberies. We found stolen property, and CCTV footage showed him at work in some of the hotels.

We still didn't have the other bloke, but just a week and a half later a man was detained while trying to drill a door in a Hilton hotel. We charged them both with 40 robberies, but we could have had them for hundreds. As we pieced together their operation, we realised how organised and careful they'd been. To check that no one was in the room, they placed tiny strips of plastic in each door jamb. They would then leave the door for a while. If the plastic had fallen out, they would guess that somebody had left the room. They had the drilling down to a fine art. They took about a minute to get inside the room. One of them had a tool belt and a lanyard with a magnetic strip card around his neck so that if anyone came across him at the door they would think he was the hotel maintenance dude. The paperwork for the case was like nothing I'd ever seen. It ran into thousands of pages. My case 'summary' was more than 80 pages.

Incredibly, Slavovic was released on bail, and he never showed up for trial. I placed notices with Interpol, but he'd vanished into thin air. The other bloke pleaded guilty, received a year in prison and, after his sentence, was deported back to Serbia.

We came across some other characters who weren't remotely as sophisticated as the Door Drillers. One man pretended to be hotel security at the Thistle Hotel at Marble Arch. He'd follow a lone woman to her room, then he'd knock at the door and say there had been reports of break-ins. While he was supposedly having a look around, he'd help himself to valuables. Foolishly, the hotel he consistently plundered was round the back of Marylebone nick. It didn't take long to catch him.

One gang that was professional, however, was a group of South American bag thieves who came over for the summer. There were several of them and they deployed the same tactics as police surveillance teams. Once they'd identified a mark – perhaps someone coming out of a luxury store laden with bags or someone they'd seen make an expensive purchase in a jewellery store – they'd follow them, changing the 'eye' and switching teams.

They'd then employ rudimentary tactics. If a victim got into a car, one of them would go to the rear offside wheel and slash it. As they were doing that, another member would already be engaging the victim in conversation, pointing out that there was a problem with the tyre. When the victim went round to inspect the damage with the gang member, invariably they would leave the door open. Another of the gang would use this opportunity to swipe the items. They even had the brass neck to dip the pockets of the person they were speaking to. It was quite bold.

When we arrested some of them, we found they were carrying large A4 Jiffy bags addressed to locations in South America. We learned that if they stole cash or wallets, they placed them straight into an envelope and posted them back to Colombia or wherever. These are dealt with as petty crimes, but the thieves were organised and made a huge amount of money. I once followed a whole group of seven and detained four of them.

We dealt with many employees who had been stealing stuff from the hotels where they worked, although only if the crimes were interesting or on a large scale. Some of these people I sympathised with. One guy at the Savoy had been there 22 years. He'd been nicking a silver-plate dining service. When we got to his house, we found loads of it. He hadn't sold it. It was just stored away. He gave it all back, but he lost his job and was devastated.

Given the locations and the well-heeled customers who frequented them, it was no surprise that we had a lot of interaction with prostitutes in hotels. I always found them very interesting to talk with. They were very open about what they did. One woman had a 6 Series BMW, a flat in Mayfair of her own, paid for from prostitution, and a child in private education. She calmly told me she'd continue working until her child had left school. The woman had left school with nothing and this was her way of making a better life for herself.

The Hotel Crime Unit certainly opened my eyes to the world of international crime. However, one case topped the lot.

Branded 'the world's top con man' by the media, Juan Carlos Guzmán-Betancourt was a thief like no other. The press often embellish and exaggerate details to sell a story, but in this case the reports weren't inaccurate. This guy was simply the greatest criminal I ever met. He wasn't a badass, he wasn't a gun-toting gangster and he wasn't a brash loudmouth. He was like something from a Hollywood film.

Handsome, charming, well-groomed and self-assured, Juan Carlos Guzmán-Betancourt had an incredible story. His crimes first came to light before I joined the hotel unit. Andy had been investigating a series of robberies at high-end hotels in 2000 involving a sophisticated deception. The trail had gone cold, however, and he wasn't able to crack it.

Some three years later and a few months after I joined, Andy spotted a small story in a newspaper about a con man who had been arrested in France for similar offences and was also wanted in London. He was sure it was the same guy.

Parisian CID had arrested him stealing something from

a hotel room and he'd given the name Alejandro Cuenca. They'd let him go on bail. Not long after that we started hearing of similar offences in London.

Andy and I were investigating around six daring burglaries in several swanky Park Lane hotels. The MO and the suspect were the same each time. A man approached the front desk pretending he was a guest. He would be immaculately turned out and would explain he'd lost his key. Once he'd blagged his way into a room, he would call security and tell them that he had forgotten his safe code. Taking huge advantage of the mantra that the customer is always right – a principle to which these institutions adhere – he knew that he would rarely be challenged as long as he was convincing enough. He helped himself to cash, jewellery and on one occasion a limited-edition £15,000 Franck Muller watch from a safe. All of the victims were incredibly wealthy and what was remarkable was that they weren't massively bothered about the thefts. It was a drop in the ocean to these people.

We dug around on the Cuenca name, but our enquiries unearthed little. Then we got his fingerprints, fed them in and it came up with a new name, Cezar Ortigozo-Vera. We had video footage and evidence for some of the offences. In one incident at the Hilton, he'd used a stolen credit card to hire a limo to take him to the airport, but the trail vanished. We suspected he must have had several aliases and passports. Another name that came up was David Vieta. We put out border alerts through Special Branch but could only do them for the names we knew. It was a needle in a haystack.

Then, out of the blue, we had an incredible stroke of luck. Andy had been out drinking and was walking in Berkeley Square at nine one night. He phoned me in an excited state. 'You're not going to believe this, but I think I'm walking behind our man right now,' he said.

The suspect had a distinctive mole in the middle of his forehead and Andy had clocked it as he walked past him. I was at the nick at Marylebone and hotfooted it to join him. I got there and saw these two guys. One of them was wearing a long leather coat. I managed to get a look at his face and I thought, 'Yes, that's definitely him.'

They both went into a nearby Sainsbury's. I jumped on Juan Carlos and Andy took the other guy. Betancourt was shocked but remained calm and was polite. When I said, 'We're police,' he replied, 'Oh, how can I help you?'

I said, 'I know who you are.'

'I don't know what you mean,' he said.

'You are David Vieta, aren't you?' I asked.

'Yes,' he said.

'Yes, but you are also Juan Carlos Guzmán-Betancourt, Alejandro Cuenca, Cezar Ortigozo-Vera.' When I reeled off all the names, I could see the colour drain from his face. 'You are under arrest,' I said.

The other guy was a bloke he'd met in a club and they were living together. He clearly had nothing to do with the scams or Guzmán-Betancourt's other aliases. We let the other man go.

We searched a house where he was living in Marylebone and found a treasure trove of evidence. Fake passports, plane tickets showing where he'd been and that he was due to leave for Greece two days after we arrested him, nearly all of the stolen property – you name it, we found it.

He was the biggest criminal we'd ever dealt with. He didn't say anything during the interrogation. At the end of a long series of taped interviews, I gave him a chance to say why he did what he did.

He looked me right in the eye. 'You wouldn't understand,' he said, and started crying. I ended the interview there and then.

He never said another word during the whole legal process, but through his lawyer he pleaded guilty to 16 of the burglaries. That was a big result for us.

It might sound strange for a police officer to say this about a habitual criminal, but Andy and I were amazed by his professionalism. He got caught not by our great detective work but through luck. Our paths just happened to cross.

When you charge someone, you have an opportunity to write pointers or markers of interest on the files, which are archived on the police databases. I wrote, 'Do not believe anything he says. He speaks several languages fluently and is a consummate liar. He will try and manipulate law enforcement officials to his own end.'

It was the first time we had to deal with media. We were quite overwhelmed by the attention, but it was good to get the recognition because we had put in a great deal of hard work.

When news of his arrest broke, it emerged that the 33-year-old Colombian was believed to have stolen more than $1 million from hotels around the world, including £150,000 in Britain. It transpired that he had at least ten identities and was wanted in Canada, Colombia, Venezuela, Mexico, Japan, Russia and Thailand.

He had first come to the attention of the authorities in Miami, when he was found, aged 13, standing on the runway at the airport. He claimed to be an orphan who had arrived in Florida by clinging onto the undercarriage of an aircraft from Colombia. His story generated widespread attention and sympathy, and a fund was created for him to live on in the United States. When he disappeared with the cash, it emerged that he was really seventeen and had two very healthy parents. For the next 16 years, he travelled the world, living the high life, conning his way from hotel to hotel, country to country.

After we finally caught him, he was sentenced to three and a half years in prison but served only two months at Standford Hill open prison on the Isle of Sheppey before, astonishingly, given his track record, he was allowed out on his own for a dental appointment. Unsurprisingly, he never returned. Police in Dublin picked him up a few weeks later for theft. Yet, despite the notes I'd made on his file, a judge felt pity for him and let him go. It didn't take long for him to disappear again.

He was then detained by US border guards after a tip-off as he waited for a taxi at a petrol station in a small town on the Canadian border. He tried to persuade the officials that he had wandered across the frontier accidentally after his car broke down. But the border guards took him into custody as a suspected illegal immigrant, until his fingerprints revealed him as the world's greatest con man. I understand he remains in prison in the US.

It's not often as a policeman that you get to meet a criminal of that calibre. He was very much like Frank Abagnale, the con man immortalised in the film *Catch Me If You Can*, in that he did it not for the money but for the thrill.

I'd love to meet him again to try to understand what made him tick.

11

GOING DEEP

AFTER MORE THAN SEVEN YEARS OF TEST PURCHASE work, I thought it was time for a change. I had already started the long-drawn-out selection procedure to go on the national undercover course, but I was beginning to get somewhat bored with doing TP jobs. I wasn't getting the same buzz I had felt at the beginning and the actions of going out, buying crack and heroin, talking in the ridiculous 'street' accent had become wearingly familiar. There was little excitement in traipsing around cold council estates any more, stinking of dirt and piss, trying to ingratiate myself with 18-year-old 'shotters'.

To make my TP deployments slightly more interesting, I decided to create 'Russian Chris', a new persona I adopted, and a nod to the glut of Eastern European immigrants in London. For this character, I decided to adopt a fake Russian accent, which would have been utterly comical had the situations not been so serious. Listening back to recordings of phone calls to dealers, I must say that it sounded blatantly awful.

Still, it kept me amused for a while, until I made a call to a Somali drug dealer in Greenwich. I had already bought from this gang several times and harboured no apprehension about calling again and then meandering up to the council flat from where they dealt.

'Yeah?'

'Er, hello, is anyfink about?' I asked in my best Russian voice.

'Who the fuck is this?' asked the young lad

'It is Chris. Russian Chris.'

'Listen, blud, wha' the fuck you talking like that for? I know you're fucking English, blud. What the fuck you talking all fucking bait for, blud?' he said.

Vociferously, I replied, 'How dare you tek the piss from my voice. *Yob tvoyu mat', sukasin.*'

'Whatever, blud. Just fuck off with your stupid fuckin' voices, fam,' he said, and put the phone down.

'Whoops,' I thought. That was the end of Russian Chris. I told the operational team, who suggested just going down to the flat to see if I could score directly. I agreed. I had nothing to lose. An hour later, I tapped on the kitchen window of the council flat in Greenwich. It was in the middle of a depressing estate and this window had a delightful view over a railway line.

The window opened and a 17-year-old black lad said, 'What?'

Still in Russian Chris mode, I asked for 'one and one' (one rock of crack and one wrap of heroin).

'Are you taking the fuckin' piss, blud?' he said. He turned to face someone inside the flat, shouting, 'It's that fucking Albanian, fam.'

I was lucky no one had yet decided to use Russian-sounding meerkats as a marketing campaign for car insurance averts or I would have been given a right doing.

Another young lad appeared at the window, smiling.

'Blud, I told you on the fuckin' phone stop talking in that fuckin' voice.'

'Is not voice,' I said. 'I don't know what you mean.'

'Blud, you are testing me. You want some fuckin' white, you come in here and fuckin' get it, blud. Come on, you can have a smoke with us,' he said grinning.

'No. My friend, he wait for me.'

'Well, listen, go and get your fuckin' friend and then come back, you fuckin' prick.'

'No. I want some now,' I said, trying to stand my ground.

'Blud, I'll come and fuckin' merk you if you don't fuck off away from me right now.' He was getting angry now.

'OK, OK,' I said. 'I come back with friend.'

Deciding discretion was the better part of valour, I left the estate and returned to the operational team empty-handed. It was a significant moment, however. I decided there and then that I'd had enough of TP work. I felt I must have been getting too old and fat to do this any more.

There were other reasons the TP work had started to lose its appeal. The focus of the operations had begun to shift. Before, we'd used the connection with the street dealer to lead us to the bigger players and greater arrests, larger seizures and a feeling we were effecting damage on a criminal network. These days, though, we were simply settling for the junkie.

We'd be giving them £5 extra to entice them, or we would let them take the gear for themselves. We weren't quite performing the role of agent provocateur, but it was on the line. Everything we did was, of course, backed by law, but I felt that morally we were getting into a grey area. I began to feel uncomfortable that, in a statistics-driven environment, we were starting to lose focus on what was important. I thought we weren't targeting the people we should have been. It was all about getting heads on sticks.

For a while, I was put in charge of a drugs intelligence office for Westminster. I wanted to make sure we didn't criminalise those we shouldn't, but inevitably the low-level dealers – people I considered victims as much as the desperate junkies they served – would get caught up in the net. It became doubly frustrating when I saw how futile it was.

Another illustration of this obsession with results was when we started targeting mobile-phone thefts. We test purchase officers would take five new mobiles, with a 200 quid price tag at retail, go into down-at-heel shops in Tottenham and say, 'Does anybody want to buy a phone for 20 quid?'

The idea was that the buyers would get done for attempting to handle stolen goods, a spurious offence if ever there was one. Unsurprisingly, there were a few takers. I used to wonder, though, whether you wouldn't get the same response had you taken the same phones into a police canteen and asked the same question. I'm sure loads of coppers would say, 'Yeah, all right.'

The end result often didn't justify the expense of the operation. We investigated one Turkish café that had a problem with cannabis dealers. I was sent to sell the owner 500 new Nokia phones and we connected with the dealers. The operation was, to all intents and purposes, a success. We achieved our objectives, but the sentences were laughable. Defence solicitors were getting wise to the TP tactic and began standing up in court saying the only reason their client went along with the ruse was to feed his habit. Where people once received prison terms of four to six years, they now got off with suspended sentences or community service.

The risks were outweighing the rewards. Since word was spreading that TP was a common tactic, I wondered how long it would take before a copper found himself in a compromising situation he couldn't get out of. The urban myth that an undercover officer cannot lie if asked directly whether he is a policeman is exactly that – a myth – but still. It was only a matter of time.

It was changed days from when TP work had been fun, when it took me to other parts of the country, not just London. One assignment in Bridgend in Wales was particularly entertaining. I was part of a team tasked to infiltrate the town's drug community and find out who the main players were. The town had a big heroin problem, as many in the provinces do, and drugs were responsible for a rise in other street crime and robberies.

It turned out the main guy was a black guy and we bought gear from him on the first day. The team was really pleased. We kept going in and buying, spending five or six hours at a time. We were being successful, but it was proving difficult for us to maintain a false identity. We had to rely on our wits. We didn't have anything in the way of logistical support and we had to have a reason for being there. Some people we were dealing with were stranger-aware and growing suspicious of our motives.

On one occasion, we had a boot full of designer clothes. The town bully was a ginger-haired bloke who got wind of the counterfeit gear, approached us one day, took loads of clothes out of the car and walked off. I followed him into a nearby pub at 11 a.m. – a big mistake, I was soon to discover, as there were about 11 of his mates, one of whom shut the door behind me. It was like something out of the Wild West. As all these guys stood around menacingly tapping pool cues against their palms, the bully bloke said,

'These clothes belong to me now and anything else I want you have to give to me.'

Just as I was thinking it was all getting a bit hairy, he punched me in the face. If I didn't think it before, I thought then I'd better get out of there. My mate Ernie had no idea where I was and I didn't want to get my head staved in for a couple of pairs of counterfeit jeans. I made my excuses while at the same time trying to maintain character. 'You Welsh cunts. I'm going to firebomb this pub,' was among the choice threats I lobbed at them while making for the door.

Only when I was outside the pub did I realise I'd caught the ringleader offering to swap some jeans for heroin on the device I was wearing. It was enough for the local police to arrest him for offering to supply drugs. He got seven years for that one offence, and that was after he'd pleaded guilty. I'd never heard anything like that. I think the magistrate had suffered some drug-related tragedy and had a zero-tolerance attitude. Plus the guy's previous conviction list was horrendous. He'd once gone into to a new pub and broken the landlord's legs in order to ram home his message that he and his mates wouldn't be paying for anything from then on.

It was a successful outcome to a long operation. In all, we must have been there for three months, working three days a week. Although we'd caught a big fish, we caught some tiddlers in the net too. One busker in the town made the silly mistake of giving us a tiny bit of cannabis resin and he got charged for supplying us that. It showed how the police everywhere were obsessed with heads on sticks. It was a really good operation, however, a totally different experience from working in London.

Although the results got some media coverage and reports

in the papers, the job caused some issues with my management back in London because it took me away from the day job for so long. I'd make sure to flag up the good press, but their attitude would always be 'What are you doing for us?'

Working for a different force didn't go down well with my inspector. I'd email my superiors and fill them in on what I'd been up to, but they didn't really give a shit, to be honest.

Sometimes you felt you couldn't win. I'd feel I had to work doubly hard on the day job to make up for it. Not surprisingly, I continued to suffer my now trademark headaches on jobs like these.

I did other out-of-town TP jobs, like buying crack and heroin for Sussex Police down on the coast. That was more difficult than it was in London. At least in the capital there were places where you just had to take a walk down the street and people would ask you what you wanted.

After five years, I'd started getting bored. 'I shouldn't be doing this so easily, it's becoming second nature to be buying crack and heroin, almost like I'm becoming a junkie.' That was what I felt like. I started doing silly things to amuse the operational team and myself.

I did a couple more operations (nice easy ones in the West End) before calling John, the TP coordinator, and telling him I was hanging up my battered Reebok Classics for good, to concentrate on my undercover course. I had bought all sorts of gear, in all different situations, worked all over the country, bought and sold stolen goods, been robbed, earned a generous amount of overtime, and had enough anecdotes and stories to fill two books. It had been a good run. I had earned a deserved reputation as a good, reliable test purchase officer.

Throughout my time as a TPO, I was encouraged to apply for undercover training. Many had tried and failed. Of course, Adrian applied and failed the course before he left the police to emigrate to Australia. In a way, I thought I owed it to him to do it. It's not for everyone, and I became living proof that unsuitable officers can get through the stringent application procedures. I put off thoughts of going for it for many years, until the desire to be one of the SO10 big boys overwhelmed me. I was a bit sick of being treated as a second-class citizen as a TPO, which is generally how they are viewed in the SO10 office. In the end, however, I had delayed it so long that I received a bit of an ultimatum from one of the guys at SO10. He basically told me that if I didn't attend the next available course I'd have to resit the entire selection procedure again because I'd waited so long.

The national undercover course is generally considered to be the police equivalent of SAS training – certainly not because the physical requirements are comparable, but because of the mental and emotional fortitude required. Students from all over the UK as well as foreign police, military and security services attend one of only two or three courses held each year.

The application and selection procedure is rightly very rigorous, although there exists a substantial element of 'it's not what you know but who you know'. In theory, candidates, regardless of their previous police experience, go through a 20-odd-page application form, a local force interview, a barrage of psychometric tests, a psychological assessment and a final interview with senior officers from across the UK. And that's just to get on the course.

In reality, some flaws exist. The psychological screening uncovers issues which you can simply say are in the process of being rectified in the psychological interview – this assures the interviewer that the issues are being dealt with. It's easy to lie as well. Maybe they expect that. After all, UCOs are trained liars.

I felt that I scraped through the whole process purely because of my language skills, especially with East European organised crime on the rise. Unlike most of those who applied for the course, I would never fit into the standard-issue 30-something shaven-headed gangster stereotype.

Eventually, I accepted a place in November 2010. I had to create a life story about who I was claiming to be, a 'legend'. For obvious reasons, it had to mirror reality as much as possible – who would want to get caught out in a lie when dealing with nasty gangsters?

You have to remember that this was the elite, the pinnacle. The story had to be believable, from birth, and had to culminate in you being a mid- or top-level criminal. First name, date of birth, place of birth remained the same as the real ones. The amount of research people put in was amazing. Part of mine was that I'd lived and worked in France and used to run drugs on the train between France and Holland. Some of the others on the same course as me had also adopted the Netherlands, so before training started three of us went over there at our own expense. I spent two days in Europe familiarising myself with the journeys and routes I said I had used, and I made sure that my legend linked in with those of the other students.

An important part of mine was accounting for the fact I could speak Russian. I said that my parents were Russian diplomats who lived in Ukraine but that I had been brought up in UK. I pretended they had both died in 1984, which was quite ingenious, I thought. That was the year of the Chernobyl nuclear disaster and few records were kept of the people who had died then, so anyone who went searching to expose holes in my story might encounter a reasonable explanation why the documentation didn't exist. In addition to this, I joined online forums and posted questions about finding details about my parents.

I had to base myself somewhere in London where, if successful, I would go 'legend-building', which essentially is taxpayer-funded beer-drinking sessions – because it's obviously very important to have a local pub to drink in where everyone knows you, or so the thinking of SO10 went.

To give me even more credibility, and to cement my legend even further, I even had a tattoo on my arm, a scroll with a Russian inscription, 'My Beautiful Mother', in homage to my fictional deceased Russian mum. Don't get me wrong, it's a nice tattoo, but it just goes to show the dedication and drive I had to be one of the SO10 gang. The legends were submitted beforehand. We had no idea if or when we would be challenged on them.

The course is shrouded in mystery, and students (successful or otherwise) never generally speak about the content. I mean, I'm not going to give any of the 'secrets' away either, but suffice to say that myths abounded. One of them was that it was necessary to dress appropriately, so, keen to impress the instructors (all SO10 detective sergeants from the office, most of whom I knew and none of whom necessarily liked me), I forked out money I didn't have on Gucci loafers, Ralph Lauren shirts and a Gieves & Hawkes blazer.

Suitably attired but woefully underprepared, as I was to find out, I arrived at Hendon training school with a hold-all full of clothes, two weeks' worth of Golden Virginia and a tummy full of butterflies.

If I thought there would be a gentle breaking in to the

course, or perhaps an explanation of how the following two weeks would pan out, I was wrong. It was straight into the work.

In all honesty, I cannot remember too many specifics about the course once it got under way. Throughout, students are subjected to intensive questioning about case law and policies, and given dozens of role-plays and cameos to do, as well as running pretend UC operations real time. It is extremely intensive, with the demands made of the students taking a substantial toll.

I existed almost solely on nicotine and caffeine. I ate very little and lost almost a stone in two weeks (if only I could do that now!). It was expected that students go to bed around 2 a.m., often after being compelled to drink beer with the staff after the final lessons in the evening, and sometimes role-plays and operations would continue through the night. I remember going to bed one day at 5 a.m. We would always have to be back in the classroom for about 8 a.m. We had maybe five or six hours' sleep a night and the weekend brought no respite at all. We were given a plethora of tasks to complete at home, some of which necessitated travelling across London or making phone calls at midnight.

Students would be dismissed from the course without ceremony. No reason would be given to the other students. They simply would not see their classmate again. Students were constantly the subject of abuse and negativity. I think being called a 'cunt' and told that you are 'useless' had a big impact on some, me included.

It was bloody hard. I make no bones about it. I think it was the hardest training I have ever undertaken. I go on training courses now and not a single one fills me with any apprehension, nerves or fear. I have no qualms about any course after experiencing the UC training.

At the beginning of the second week, I threw in the towel. I broke down in tears and told my student colleagues that I was going home. This was on a Tuesday morning.

It was getting too much for me. The constant pressure, the continual bollockings, the deep-seated belief that, after putting myself through this, I might not be good enough to make it in SO10 all drove me to the conclusion that I should just bail out.

Despite pleas from my classmates not to leave, I was determined. I didn't bother going into the classroom but grabbed Pascal, one of my tutors, as he walked into the classroom block. He told me not to leave. Obviously, he was persuasive, because, despite my wobble, I stayed on the course. Somehow, trapped in the magnetic field of SO10 again, my thoughts of leaving disappeared after a positive word from one of the instructors, which, in my head, I interpreted as almost a guarantee of passing.

Later that day, it was my turn for a grilling on my legend. I gingerly sat in the chair, ready for my interrogation. Initially, it went OK and I managed to bat a lot of the questions away. I think I had done my research fairly well. They started asking me about prices of drugs and I began floundering. They laughed at my answers and I could feel myself sinking.

'So you know Amsterdam?' asked Joe, one of the interrogators.

'Yeah, pretty well,' I said. I was confident because I had been there only a couple of weeks before to prepare for this very scenario.

'What's the name of the main canal?' he demanded.

Blank. 'Er, I dunno,' I said.

'What about the main street?' he asked.

Again, all the streets and information I thought I had committed to memory just simply weren't there. 'I've forgotten,' I said.

'And the main square? What's that called?' he said.

Christ, I thought. I've fucked this. 'Er, can't remember,' I replied.

'Hmm, you're a bit of a fucking bullshitter, aren't you?' Joe said.

'Big Billy Bullshitter,' said Pascal, the other interrogator.

'No, not at all,' I replied calmly, sensing they were moving in for the kill.

'Speak Russian, do you?' demanded Pascal.

'Yeah, a bit,' I said. I heard some muttering from my classmates. I was tested on my language skills and managed to be impressive enough for the class to erupt into applause.

I can't talk much about the course, as the details are classified, but suffice to say it was gruelling. As we neared the end, I was mentally exhausted.

On the day after the final exercise, they told us we had all passed. There was no ceremony, no clapping of hands, but that night everyone went out for a meal in a local restaurant. In keeping with the general tone of the course, the instructors used the after-dinner speeches to poke fun at the students. When they turned their attention to me, they read out what they claimed was an excerpt from my diary of the course. I have to admit it was vaguely amusing. They thought I was a posh, sensitive type and it was all 'woe is me' type stuff.

Feeling relaxed – and braver – because those who remained had all passed, I started slagging the instructors off. I finished by saying, 'Right, I'm now off to get my standard-issue Stone Island jacket and crew cut and make the transformation into an east London gangster.'

You could almost see the tumbleweed drift past. Some of the instructors looked genuinely offended. I could scarcely believe it. After all the bollockings they had dished out over the past two weeks, they suddenly revealed themselves to be thin-skinned. If you can't take it, don't give it out, I always say.

Of the twelve that had originally started the course, eight passed. Of these, six joined undercover teams in the UK, while two were from foreign forces. Like many of my fellow students, I joined the part-time index. This system operated much like the test purchasing. It meant you were available for undercover work but you performed these duties alongside your day job. One woman on the course went straight into the Full-Time Undercover Unit. It showed how in demand female operatives were.

I had made it. I was part of the elite. There was nothing else to do but wait in anticipation for a job. A couple of weeks later, I got my first role.

12

PARK LANE GRUB

ELATED. THAT WAS HOW I FELT AFTER PASSING MY undercover course. I went about my day job in the drugs unit with a new sense of purpose. I certainly wouldn't say that I now had the requisite ego, but I did feel a cut above the rest, I must admit.

In any case, I set about my post-course tasks with glee. I made sure I was first in the queue to fill out the application forms for my new undercover identity documents – a passport, driver's license and credit card in my pseudonym, Christian Gregorovich Sulyenko.

To complement my extremely tongue-in-cheek choice of fake name, I conjured up more intricate fantastical back stories about him – I mean, me.

However, it was long before my new documents arrived that I was assigned my first undercover job, and it was as far away from lice-infested crack houses as you could get!

I had a call from Jane, one of the cover officers in the ivory tower of the SO10 office, asking me to attend a briefing there that afternoon. I hurriedly explained to my detective sergeant what was going on and hopped onto a bus from Park Lane down to Victoria.

Suddenly, the excitement I'd felt only moments before turned to nerves, and I was as jittery as I'd been on my first test purchase job in Haringey. And so it was with a modicum of trepidation that I nervously knocked at the hallowed door of the SO10 office.

'What the fuck are you knocking for, you prick?' shouted Dave, one of the instructors from my course. 'You're one of us, now – you don't need to knock.'

'Oh,' I muttered, fumbling and embarrassed, like I was chatting up a girl at a school disco or something. 'Is Jane here?'

'In there,' said Dave, nodding towards a smaller room where briefings were held.

I knocked on the door, which had been locked from the inside. In the room, I sat and glanced around. Orv, a black officer I had worked with as a TPO, was there, and he smiled a greeting.

Jane, her face thunderous, said, 'Where the fuck have you been? I said one o'clock.'

Her scowl and caustic Scouse tones told me I had made a booboo. It was 2 p.m. by my watch. Whoops. 'Shit, sorry,' I said.

'Well, we've been waiting for you for fucking ages. The DI [she gestured towards a well-groomed three-piece-suit-clad chap in the corner] needs to go somewhere.'

'Sorry, guv,' I said to the none-too-impressed detective inspector. He mumbled an acceptance and said, 'Let's crack on, shall we?'

And so my introduction to the undercover world had already singled me out for my reliability. Not. In any case, we had a quick briefing and I was told literally nothing about the background to the operation. All I knew was that I was to be at Heathrow Airport a bit later that day, about

6 p.m. Orv and the target of the operation (the baddie) would meet me. My role was to be a diamond dealer working for a major criminal gang. We would drive to Hatton Garden, London's jewellery heartland, and make a quick pit stop before driving further to one of Park Lane's grandest hotels to meet the rest of the 'gang' – a host of other undercover officers. This whole operation was what they called 'theatre', an extravagant showpiece designed to fool baddies into thinking they were dealing with some 'proper' criminals.

While it wasn't exactly the sort of stuff I had envisaged getting involved in as an undercover cop, I did think it sounded like a nice easy one for my first outing.

Enthused after the briefing, I made quick arrangements with Orv about when and where to meet at the airport. He also instructed me to speak in foreign languages while in the presence of the baddie. He thought it would impress him further.

I had to sort out the minor things that applied to all undercover jobs. I inserted a brand new SIM card into a spare Blackberry I had and gave Jane and Orv the number. This wasn't some fancy Met-issue card, but a random SIM bought at a newsagent's somewhere. The only precaution we took was not to buy SIM cards from anywhere in the vicinity of Scotland Yard, just in case the worst happened and they could be traced to a retailer.

I hadn't given much thought to the equipment at our disposal in SO10, but I guess if I had I would have expected it to be cutting edge. This was the elite, after all. But when Jane handed me my audio recording device, I'm afraid it was more Johnny English than James Bond. I suppose you could argue that at least it didn't look like a tape recorder, but the truth was it was rubbish. If anything, it drew attention to itself because you would want to ask, 'What's that?' if you saw it. Helpfully, for a covert recording device, it had a little red button that said 'Record'. And another that said 'Stop'.

I didn't have any choice but to take it. I tried to put it out of my mind as I went to Heathrow. I rendezvoused with my fellow undercover officer, Orv, and the target, a man suspected of being involved in assassinations. The undercover officer had been working on it for months.

We went to Hatton Garden and, en route, I spoke in Russian over my phone to add weight to the story that I was an international diamond dealer. After a brief stop-off at a jeweller's, and accompanied by some more in-car linguistic theatre (this time in French), we traversed central London in Orv's stylish Audi coupé. We eventually ended up at the Grosvenor House Hotel in Mayfair.

It was only when we arrived at the hotel that I started to panic. Given that I had worked for three years for the Hotel Crime Unit, I worried that someone from a security department would recognise me. The Grosvenor House Hotel had been a regular haunt for Andy and me in those days. I knew all of the security team by sight. Not only that, but someone might remember me from my time as a beat bobby in Mayfair. Hundreds of times I had hidden round by the staff entrance, chatting to waiters, bellboys, chambermaids and receptionists, desperate to relieve the boredom of interminable security patrols in Park Lane. I began to question why SO10 had brought me here when they must have known there was a risk of identification. It's not like they're not fully aware of where everyone has worked. SO10 were potentially putting this whole huge ongoing operation at risk.

Still, as the new face, I tried to relax into the role. But

my mind was buzzing. In the hotel, we sat down in the champagne bar and ordered some bubbly. More undercover officers showed up, under various guises. There was a lot of East End gangster chat going on – not exactly my scene. I pretended not to be following their conversation and concentrated on staying in character for the benefit of the target. He only stuck around for about 20 minutes in the bar. Soon, he made his excuses and left. I thought that would signal the end of this piece of theatre. I was wrong.

There were four of us left in the bar. Soon, however, another chap from SO10 showed up. The other officers were ordering £100 of champagne. The five of us then went for a huge slap-up meal, which cost about a grand.

I could appreciate the need to keep the pretence of us being big spenders going, but the money being spent was astounding. I was pissed as a fart. When it came time to go home, they were all saying, 'Don't worry about it. Never pay for anything. It's always the firm that pays.' I was living in Fulham at the time and got a taxi, which again I was urged to claim on expenses.

In the morning, I was worried about the extent of the spending and, keen to make sure it didn't rebound on me, rang the cover officer asking if I should pay for it. He said, 'Nah, we'll cover that. It's an expense, just submit it.'

I downloaded the recording, put it in an evidence bag and wrote up my notes. I'd taken my first steps into the world of undercover policing.

13

PENETRATION TESTING

DURING MY FIRST FORAYS INTO UNDERCOVER POLICING, 'The firm always pays for everything' was an oft-repeated mantra. Essentially, the unwritten rule was that as soon as you were deployed on a UC operation (including travelling to and from the job) you were undercover, and therefore not liable for any daily expenses, minutiae such as a Starbucks double tall skinny latte included.

This suited me fine and, apart from that first time, I never questioned the ethics of it. Although I should have done, I suppose. I was introduced to the archaic expenses system in SO10: filling out a form by hand and getting it signed by the DI. There were different boxes to tick depending on what the expenditure was. It was incredibly and unnecessarily complex, old-fashioned and, for people who used several different identities, extremely confusing. The expenses system was to be a harbinger of doom for me.

In the meantime, though, I was enjoying my sporadic part-time undercover exploits. At the same time as running my own test purchase operations in my day job in central London, after work I would go and operate undercover for SO10, with the occasional overnight job.

One such job was, I thought, bizarre in the extreme. Under the operational requirement that went by the innuendo-laden moniker of 'penetration testing', I found myself with two other UCs and a detective sergeant cover officer, Dave, in an anonymous (but comfortable) hotel in the south-west of England.

Eager for my briefing, I was all ears as Dave (in his typically SO10 south-east London gangster drawl) told us that our job was to infiltrate the police headquarters of a large southern English force. I won't name them to spare them the embarrassment. Suffice to say that an issue had been identified with the perimeter security at the HQ and that security staff were not doing their job.

We were instructed to find as many ways as possible of getting into the HQ complex and, once inside, make our way to the canteen or another large communal area and leave items behind – just innocuous-looking boxes and suchlike. It was potentially a serious matter, but I would never have dreamed we'd be doing anything like this at all!

We had a very short meeting with the assistant chief constable of the force, who handed us each a personally signed letter, which we were to show if we were challenged having infiltrated the HQ. It basically said that the holder was engaged in a covert exercise and that the recipient of the letter should call a mobile number in bold type at the end of the missive. This was the personal mobile number of the assistant chief.

I, along with the other two UCs – Kath, a flaxen-haired Londoner, and Diggory, a diminutive Northern Irishman – spent two days blagging our way into the supposedly secure police headquarters complex. We walked in brazenly through the rear gates, the favoured egress and entry for those having a quick fag break. I forged a car park pass, using a marker pen and the back of an envelope, and happily breezed into a space. Kath and I wandered around unchecked, drinking a cuppa in the canteen and leaving an empty, nondescript box under our table, with the word 'bomb' written on it. Diggory hid in the boot of a BMW 7 Series, which I drove into the complex, pretending to be a dithery, halfwit posh boy unfamiliar with the area. I was beckoned into the car park by security and allowed to turn my car round to go back the way I had came. Once we were inside the complex, Diggory got out of the boot and, brandishing a DeWalt toolbox, wandered around the HQ. Incredibly, when he met up with us later, he told us that a firearms instructor who thought he was there to fix a window had actually showed him round the armoury! Unbelievable.

As we were there for two days, during the evening we enjoyed sumptuous meals and drinks (all paid for by the job, natch), and we even went out drinking and clubbing in the nearest town. I happily started a whip-round, sticking in 40 quid of my own money, only to have it thrust back into my hand with the comment, 'Never pay for anything with your own money, son.' Confused, I began to protest, saying that technically we had finished the operation for the day and so weren't 'on the job', or deployed on the operation. We were enjoying a drink and a boogie after work, surely? Not according to my comrades, we weren't.

In my day job, I was struggling to get funding to combat drug dealing, yet they're quite happy to sign off £500 for a nightclub. The idea was that you were never a cop, you were always in role. But you would always sit there talking about work, because cops can't talk about anything but work.

Still, as the newbie, I happily indulged and, although

slightly uncomfortable about it, put it to the back of my mind. Dave, who was a hilarious individual, had me in stitches in this hideous provincial nightclub, dad-dancing to commercial house and dance tracks, much to the disgust of the local meatheads.

After a heavy night, which involved a kebab and a drunken taxi back to the hotel, I rose the next morning with a throbbing cranium but also amusing memories and a fair amount of happiness that I was beginning to get into this UC scene. I could quite easily do this for a living, I thought. It was great.

No sooner had Diggory dropped me back home later that day than I had a phone call about my next expedition. I was tasked with trying to buy cocaine from some Kosovan gangsters.

For this task, I was adopting the persona of Kristoforas Starszewski, a criminal mastermind with a vast stolen goods empire spanning two continents. My multilingual skills were again going to be put to the test as I paved the way for a significant drug bust. To gain a bit of credence amongst the gangsters, I was, once again, to ensure that I indulged in some Russian repartee on the phone in the presence of the Kosovan baddies. I often got the impression that Eastern European gangsters were all lumped into the same boat, with an assumption that if I spoke Russian there would be some sort of commonality between us. Obviously, nothing could be further from the truth. Linguistically, Russian and Albanian are worlds apart; indeed, they exist in totally different linguistic hemispheres, with Albanian having more in common with Finnish. Still, I was just happy to oblige and do as ordered. I often felt more comfortable with foreign criminals, as I knew I could gain a bit more credibility if I spoke a foreign language.

Mr Starszewski favoured greased back hair, in a ponytail, with baggy jeans, a short-sleeved T-shirt and box-fresh Reeboks. I thought I looked rather like a paedophile, and indeed I purloined this crime-against-fashion look for a future operation against one. Starszewski was a hands-on villain, running his organisation at the sharp end, hence the casual look.

I picked up the designated car, which, for this job, was that stalwart of the fun-loving criminal, a Honda CR-V – more Home Counties family car than homeboy. Ah, well. We arrived at our rendezvous, which, as was usual, took place in a particularly undesirable area of east London. My hands were clammy as I clumsily parked the car in a busy side street. Mike made a call to the baddie and we waited. And waited. After we'd been waiting an hour, a young Kosovan appeared. He was dressed as if he was out for the evening at the Roadhouse in Covent Garden. Fashionably distressed jeans, a gaudy Versace-esque T-shirt and terribly pointy leather shoes. The intense odour of Davidoff Cool Water aftershave filled the interior of our family SUV as he got in and sat in the front passenger seat.

We introduced ourselves and I saw him take in everything in the car, mentally noting the CDs, the rubbish, the coffee cups. He was evidently a switched-on cookie. Once we got down to the business in hand, the meeting went swimmingly. The baddie joined us and we had a chat. As usual, the actual business end of the chat lasted seconds. The rest of the conversation was niceties and small talk. I 'received' a phone call during the meeting and spoke Russian. He looked fairly astonished. I am pretty sure this went a long way to establishing a modicum of credibility for me. We parted company after only 15 minutes or so. It was only after he got out of the car that I noticed two Audis which had been parked parallel with us pull away almost instantly. I have no doubt that this was his 'security' team.

I met him again a couple of weeks later. It was an eye-opener. They almost had a surveillance team, blocking off the street, making sure we weren't being followed. It was high-level sophistication. We pulled up in the same side street and made the same phone call, notifying him of our arrival. Being slightly more aware of what was going on this time, I saw five or six Albanian/Kosovan-looking dudes strolling up and down the street, and after some minutes they appeared to station themselves on the street corners, each looking in separate directions. Then, a dark-blue BMW X5 appeared and stopped at the junction with the main road, hazards flashing, as if broken down. At the junction behind us, a similar scenario was happening, this time with a black Audi. They had literally boxed off the street. They had closed it down and they had it under complete surveillance! All this just for a meeting. These guys were taking absolutely no chances. I was dumbfounded. The professionalism these guys executed was remarkable. They were almost as impressive as the South American pickpockets and bag thieves I had once pursued. Evidently, these guys deserved their reputation as efficient and professional criminals.

This sort of activity made my heart race faster. The risks were there, and it would only take one word out of place, or one little fuck-up, and this gang would not only immediately back out of the deal but would probably also effect some sort of retribution. They had a rep to maintain.

Another guy involved was, I have to say, phenomenal. While he loved to blah his way in the office, with tall stories and incredible tales, he was probably one of the few people for whom these tales were absolutely true. His, ahem, assertive stance with these Kosovans put them on the back foot and I think they were secretly impressed to be dealing with such an evil bastard.

Obviously, that meet went fine as well, but with all the layers of protection this crew had in place, I dread to think what would have happened had the baddie discovered who we were.

That was a fairly typical SO10 job. When it came down to it, the unit delivered, and it was more like the type of stuff you read about. It was interesting and I still felt enthusiastic about it. It was a 'proper' job, the sort discussed on courses, or in the pub. I felt really pleased to have been involved. Eventually, the baddies all got busted in the midst of a multi-kilo cocaine deal, at gunpoint, by armed cops.

Despite my reservations, annoyance and compounded stress levels about various logistical problems, I was still proud and enthusiastic. This was the sort of job I had envisaged doing, and with such great results who could be bothered by the minutiae of silly little problems?

14

CASINO SCAMS AND NAKED CELEBRITIES

'MEET ME OUTSIDE THE RITZ, MATE,' SAID PHIL, ONE OF my favourite DSs in the SO10 office.

'OK. What's it about?' I asked, curiously.

'It's a casino job. I'll tell you when you get there.'

'OK,' I replied. I was intrigued.

Remembering my time on the Hotel Crime Unit, I hastily got myself suited and booted, complete with a tie. I had often been ordered by the head of security at the Ritz to use the staff entrance, as guests would not want to see a dishevelled, long-haired, jeans-wearing cop wandering through the public areas of the luxury venue!

I met Phil in Piccadilly, outside the entrance to the Ritz casino. He swiftly explained to me that the Met Gaming Unit (which investigates organised gambling fraud) had its sights on a chap in Slough who was offering a seemingly illegal gambling scam in online adverts. To get into him, I needed a crash course in how to play roulette.

I was ushered into the Ritz's high-rollers' roulette suite, where the float was around a million pounds and, I was told, entry was solely for those expected to stake at least three million quid. An officious but knowledgeable senior croupier and a member of the casino's management gave me a five-hour crash course in playing roulette, along with a run-down of all the current scams available. Then, mentally exhausted – maths is *not* my strong point – I went with Phil to the Gaming Unit office at Charing Cross nick for a briefing.

Our target was a loner, Ricardo, who had a severe gambling habit, with a penchant for roulette. He had been advertising a seemingly foolproof scam to win cash from the computerised roulette machines ubiquitous in casinos and betting shops all over the land. He frequented a casino in Slough. The team thought he might have had illegal access to programmes for the machines or possess some sort of cheating device.

Later that night, issued with a top-of-the-range Volvo, dressed up in a Gieves & Hawkes suit and Gucci loafers, with a grand in cash and Christian Sulyenko's driving licence in my Prada wallet, I went to the casino in Slough. A virgin when it came to this sort of thing, I was expecting a James Bond-esque palatial affair; I thought I'd be mingling with gangsters' molls and tuxedoed villains. As it was, it was more like being a guest on *The Jeremy Kyle Show*, with inbred buffoons (some wearing tracksuits and trainers, for God's sake) and fag-smoking harridans. Slightly disappointed but still with the job in mind, I spent a few hours there aimlessly gambling taxpayers' cash, not really winning anything back and, despite my keen eye, not actually seeing our target.

The next day, the operational team gave me Ricardo's mobile number and I called him asking to have a bit of this great money-making opportunity. We arranged to meet up in a hotel bar in Leicester Square and then go on to the casino there so he could show me the scam in detail.

Nervous, I sipped a cappuccino in the well-appointed bar as hotel staff and guests milled around. I was approached by a weedy-looking boy who I initially thought was about 16. He looked like he could do with a good dose of sunshine. Too much PlayStation, I fleetingly considered. Incredibly, he introduced himself as Ricardo. Shocked, although obviously not showing it, I shook his clammy, feeble hand and offered him a drink. He declined and nervously perched on the edge of a leather armchair while he took me through the rudiments of his cheating system.

To be honest, I had no fucking idea what he was on about. It was utter gobbledegook. The guy, I thought, was a loser, and possibly a bit of a nutter. I suggested going to the casino so he could show me the scam in action.

We strolled across Leicester Square and into the casino, where we sat at a bank of roulette machines. He asked me for £20 to put in the machine and then painstakingly went through every move. Even with my lack of mathematical skills, I was utterly dumbfounded. The 'scam' was not a cheat or a system at all. It merely involved placing a stake on nearly every number. What a load of bollocks. Feigning enthusiasm and naivety, I asked him how much investment he wanted.

'Five grand,' he said, completely deadpan. 'And I'll double it within a month.'

'Is he serious?' I thought. 'He is having a laugh.'

'Mate,' I said, my gangster persona kicking in, 'I could double five grand in an hour, dealing in the sort of shit I deal with.'

I felt slightly sorry for him. He was dressed in cheap garb, obviously had lots of issues and wasn't an overly bad person, just a bullshitter.

'Let me think about it,' I said, getting up to leave. This

was a waste of time, I thought, and it was an appropriate moment to end this particular job. Crestfallen, he agreed, and I walked him back to his car, a beaten-up black Toyota with Berkshire Council taxi livery on it. The guy was a fucking cabbie! Eager to part ways with this waste of space, I bade him farewell, this time not even shaking his hand. And then he said, 'Well, I suppose I could always do that old dear in.'

Suddenly intrigued, I said, 'Whaddya mean? What old dear?'

'There's an old woman I know, she's got thousands stuffed in her mattress,' Ricardo replied. 'I'm thinking of robbing it off her, you know, tying her up and nicking it all. I've thought about it, I just need some CS gas – cos she's got a dog – and a wetsuit, you know, so I don't leave any DNA behind.'

Slightly appalled but nonetheless aware that he was planning what sounded like a criminal act, I offered my help to do this. I said I would call him a bit later on to discuss it. Momentarily buoyed by this, he seemed excited and said it would be good to have some help and advice.

Leaving him to examine the parking ticket that was attached to his windscreen, I trotted back to Charing Cross nick. Briefing the operational team, I explained that the casino scam was a no-go and a load of rubbish but that there was potential for something more sinister. Despite the fact that this guy was obviously a bullshit merchant and a bit of a Walter Mitty-type character, we were obliged to take action. We joined forces with the local police in Thames Valley, and over the course of several days I liaised with Ricardo and met with him a couple more times, with the intention of identifying the potential victim and her address so that action could be taken.

Each time I spoke or met with Ricardo, I felt slightly sick. He would go into extraordinary detail about how he intended to rob this old woman and what he intended to do with her. I offered all the help I could, including a van and equipment. Ricardo seemed like he was being egged on by my apparent enthusiasm, and he made more and more extraordinary plans, like dressing up in SAS outfits, using Tasers and killing the old woman's dog.

Obviously, Ricardo had some problems. But the most important thing was that we identified the old woman – and, yes, she did have a mattress full of cash. Arrangements were made for a low level of protective surveillance for her, just in case Ricardo decided to go it alone.

After meeting Ricardo in person and getting a final plan of the act recorded on a device, the police moved in and arrested him for conspiracy to burgle. He told them he knew I was an undercover cop – a common refrain. I don't think the case even got to court, unsurprisingly. Ricardo was just one of many poor dimwitted and down-on-their-luck individuals who were forced to cross the line into extraordinary acts by virtue of their circumstances, often debt-related. I had a certain amount of sympathy for him but knew that there was always the possibility that he would have carried out his heinous plan.

Ricardo was a bit of a buffoon, as was the target of the next operation I was involved in. Phil, who evidently had something of a penchant for giving me unusual jobs, called me into the SO10 office one afternoon.

'It's just a quick job, mate. I need you out this evening.'

'OK,' I agreed, still eager to bolster my undercover CV.

We traipsed into the meeting room in the SO10 office for a briefing with a DI from Camden police station and a female UC, Kerry. I had never worked with Kerry before, but it was clear she was more experienced in this line of work. I listened to the DI summarise the job and what he wanted.

He explained that a very famous celebrity of international acclaim had been the victim of a burglary in which her laptop had been stolen. This laptop, it transpired, contained intimate images of the celebrity, and Burglar Bill had found them. This had led to the offender contacting the celeb directly and essentially threatening to publish or sell the photos to the media unless he was paid tens of thousands of pounds – a clear-cut case of blackmail.

Kerry had already been in touch with the suspect and, posing as the client's solicitor, had arranged to meet to make the payment of £20,000 and retrieve the photographs. My role was to act as Kerry's solicitor's clerk colleague. Really, I was there to ensure her safety and corroborate any evidence she might glean. Two other UC officers had been tasked with collecting the money (and, yes, they did actually have £20,000) from the cash office upstairs and waiting round the corner to do the handover when we gave the signal.

So, four hours later, having had a bite to eat (courtesy of the job, of course), I was sitting in a nondescript VW Golf with Kerry in an anonymous Camden side street as she called our blackmail suspect. Feigning a ridiculously posh voice, she enquired where he was and explained we were in the street he had requested us to meet him in. Some verbal toing and froing ensued, and he insisted that he would not come to our car, nor would he meet us in person. He agreed to leave a USB stick with the incriminating images thereon on a nearby garden wall. This was just so we could confirm that he had them in his possession.

He was obviously nervous and wondering whether this

was some sort of set-up. The prospect of netting a cool 20 K was some motivation, however, and about 20 minutes after Kerry finished her call a hooded youth stealthily crept up to a small garden wall on our left and put a blue USB stick on the top of it.

The lad scurried off, totally unaware that a top-notch surveillance team was now tailing him. Celebs evidently get a slightly better service from the Old Bill than your usual man in the street!

So, as our chum gleefully scampered away, I got out of the car and retrieved the USB stick. Without speaking, and with some trepidation and excitement, I plugged the stick into the sterile laptop we had with us. Kerry and I were both as excited as small kids to find out the identity of the celeb – and to see these salacious pics!

I clicked on the file and opened the images. Slightly disappointed, I instantly recognised the celebrity, an individual of international repute. Far from being the blurry pornographic sex-fest we had expected, these were all tasteful artistic nude photos, with no overtly sexual overtones. As my excitement waned, I made sure I copied the photos onto the hard drive of the laptop.

The suspect called Kerry and insisted we replace the USB stick on the wall. He was evidently spooked by something and insisted that he did not want to collect the cash today. We were a bit deflated after all the hanging around as well as the preparation for the job. Still, I placed the USB stick back on the wall. Safe in the knowledge the street was under observation by the surveillance boys, Kerry and I drove back to the base.

We parked and jumped into the lift up to the SO10 office. Phil was there and, with a cheeky grin, he grabbed the laptop from me.

'Right, let's see these dirty photos, then!' he said as he booted it up.

'Mate, they're not dirty. They're actually quite boring,' I said.

'Fuck that. Let's see some minge,' he squawked excitedly.

As he scrolled through the images, it was clear Phil was disappointed.

'Fuck me. What a load of old bollocks,' he said.

He slammed the lid of the laptop shut and ordered Kerry and me to write up our evidence. She and I grinned at each other and sat down to write.

After a lengthy arrest and investigation, the suspect was charged with blackmail. He eventually got seven years in prison, which was a UK record (apparently) for a blackmail sentence.

The celebrity, whose identity I shall keep secret until I go to my grave (not least because of a court order), had, I hasten to add, nothing to be ashamed of and looked very, very good!

15

HARRY THE GRASS

'THANK YOU, MR SULYENKO,' SMILED THE CASHIER pleasantly. She handed over my gold credit card (limit: none), and I grabbed the cigarettes and the receipt from the till.

Trotting back to the car, I pondered my impending meeting. I had never been to Manchester before. I tended to avoid anywhere north, to be honest. It might have been down to the company I kept, but most of what I'd seen was a shithole. But Harry, a contact from Russia, had convinced me that it would be worth meeting up with Tayvon, who had access to, and wanted to sell, a shedload of guns.

I had met Harry in Russia while cultivating some contacts in the field of stolen electronics. Harry was from Belfast and was working in Moscow. I used to bung Harry a few quid every now and then, and he would help take delivery of one of the lorryloads of stolen iPhones that I arranged to sneak into Russia, amazingly using bent contacts in the air freight industry and in Russian customs. I would make around 20 grand on each lorryload and I made sure that Harry got a good whack. Harry was back in the UK now, trying to go slightly straight, in Manchester, but he had his fingers in a few pies. He was also well respected in the criminal fraternity for his extensive network of contacts and his reliability when it came to work. It was well known that he used to live in Russia, and he was often referred to as 'Harry the Russian'. Harry and Christian Sulyenko went way back, and their unquestionable friendship spanned many years and continents. Harry was, of course, actually a police informant.

Before calling Harry, I met up with the guys who had arranged this operation. They were from an elite unit made up of officers from several Northern forces that were targeting gunrunners and badass gangsters. After a quick briefing and a chat with my London-based cover officer, I called Harry and arranged to meet him at a well-known pub in a Manchester suburb.

I didn't like doing business in pubs and I didn't really trust informants. I wasn't much keen on dealing with guns or working alone, either. But my yearning to be 'one of the lads' overtook any misgivings I had. I knew this would be a corker of a job if it came off and that it could give me a modicum of credibility in the SO10 office. And all I had to do was meet this guy Tayvon. Of course, I had to just remember I was Christian Sulyenko, big-time criminal, with some major Eastern European contacts of very scary proportions.

Harry turned up about half an hour late. We greeted each other in Russian.

'*Privyet,*' I said.

'*Privyet, Gaspadin Sulyenko,*' Harry replied.

'*Nu, vsjo v porjadkje?*' I asked.

'*Konjeshno, konjeshno. Pit' khoctchesh?*'

'*Potchemu njet?*' I replied '*Pivo, poszhaluista.*'

Such pleasantries would hopefully satisfy any keen ears nearby. After a quick pint we got into my car and, directed by Harry, drove into my least favourite scenario.

It was dark by the time we met, and, *naturellement*, it was pissing down with rain. I didn't have a fucking clue where we were. Harry directed me down street after street after street, until he said we were nearly there. Evidently, we were in Moss Side, which I had been told could be our destination. Well, no disrespect to any law-abiding inhabitants, but it confirmed my sweeping generalisations about Northern estates. Broken glass and dogshit everywhere. Every shop had security grilles. Errant youths wearing hooded tops scowled at us from BMX bikes they'd probably nicked. The street uniform *du jour* was Adidas trainers and baggy Nike trackpants. The fear gripped me that they could smell I was a cop. If this went bent, I might not get out alive. My mind was going nineteen to the dozen. I was wondering if Harry was actually on our side or if this was a bluff of some sort to get a cop beaten up, or worse. I kept glancing at him as I drove. For such a reserved and normally collected guy, he looked fucking nervous too. This only made me more anxious.

We eventually came to a parade of shops, all derelict aside from a 24/7 newsagent-type affair at the end. It had the requisite security grille and Plexiglass-encased CCTV cameras aimed at the doorway. Hanging around in the drizzle, hazily lit by the streetlights, was a large group of young lads, all hoodies and Adidas trainers. They were mainly black and all stared at us intently. As we pulled to a halt, the car was quickly surrounded by bike-riding youngsters peering in the windows at us and pointing.

'Who the fuck is this?' said one loudly.

Another tapped on the window. 'Y'all right, mate? Who you?'

I began to wind the window down to speak, but Harry touched my arm. His eyes said 'wait'.

This had to be some sort of ambush. Then the rear passenger door opened. I spun round in my seat. Fuck, this is it.

I reached for my phone (as if that was going to be any use) while trying to maintain a semblance of calm.

A young black guy with a pockmarked face and eyes that looked like they belonged to a 60-year-old slid along the back seat.

'All right? I'm Tayvon,' he said to me, before enthusiastically greeting Harry.

Harry said, 'I'll leave you to it,' got out of the car and wandered over to the newsagent's shop.

'Who are you then?' said Tayvon.

Mindful that waffling and talking too much could spell my downfall, I said, 'I'm Chris. Harry tells me you've got some metalwork you can move.'

'Yeah, maybe. How do you know Harry?'

I explained I knew him from Russia and that I was well connected to Russians in London. All the time, Tayvon had his hands in his pockets and I knew that he was the first in a chain of contacts in a very violent and nasty gang – one that frequently liked to show off its shooting skills. As Christian Plowman, I was fucking nervous. But Christian Sulyenko was not a nervous man, I hoped.

Probably because he was quite young and the talk of foreign, glamorous gangsters overwhelmed him, Tayvon eventually grinned and said, 'Let's talk business.'

We spoke briefly. I was relieved we were at this stage without any issues. We chatted for a minute at the most.

Once the mask of his initial bravado slipped, Tayvon appeared more nervous than I was, although I still harboured fear about a potential ambush of some sort. I was still a bit wild-eyed with paranoia and I just wanted the meeting over, to be honest.

I took Tayvon's phone number and assured him one of my associates would be in touch about arranging a gun deal. We touched fists (as opposed to 'we fisted each other', which I had mistakenly written once upon a time in an evidential notebook) and Tayvon got out, joining the by now uninterested group of youths by the newsagent's.

Harry emerged from the shop, touched fists with several of the group and embraced Tayvon. He obviously knew them all, and there appeared to be a level of mutual respect between Harry and Tayvon. Harry was evidently a well-connected dude.

Still slightly terrified that I was going to be done over and end up bleeding to death in a Mancunian gutter, I willed Harry back into the car. Now the contact had been made, I wanted to get the fuck out of there. Eventually, he did get in and we drove off, wipers going, with no small relief that we were leaving this urban warzone.

Harry didn't even ask me how it went. He had done his bit. That was it. For me, it wasn't. I was still Mr Christian Sulyenko. I was Mr Sulyenko until I got back behind my own front door. I dropped Harry off at a Sainsbury's car park. Cool, calm and self-assured, he bade farewell.

I gave Tayvon's number to one of my Eastern European contacts, and as a result the local police ended up seizing a ridiculous amount of firearms, including machine guns, and nicked a shedload of Northern gangsters, Tayvon included.

I never saw Harry again. I've been told he isn't an

informant any more. He got such a good payout from the operation that he moved overseas. It wasn't for a while afterwards that the relevance of how he'd greeted me in the Manchester pub hit home.

'Hello, Mr Sulyenko,' he'd said.

How the fuck had he known my name? Did SO10 have a snitch?

16
NEVER TRUST A SNOUT

I SCOURED THE INTRANET VACANCIES SECTION, AS I DID every Thursday afternoon, more out of curiosity than anything else. My day-to-day job in central London was becoming staid and boring, and I needed a new challenge.

The management where I worked had run out of budget to give me to run complex drugs operations, and I was left alone to collate intelligence about drug dealers and the like, as well as having to attend an infuriating daily meeting. This involved about 20 people, most of whom were cops (there were a few civilians – intelligence analysts, for example), led by a DI who couldn't make his mind up about which crime issues to prioritise in our area.

Every so often, I would become so pissed off at the futility of it all that I would refuse to provide the daily statistics for which I was asked. Instead, I'd suggest that rather than stand in a meeting for an hour every morning talking bollocks we all went out on patrol and actually physically addressed the very issues we were discussing. This was always met with derision and my views were dismissed as those of some sort of immature maverick.

'Marvin,' I called out to my detective sergeant. 'Do you

know anything about this?' I asked, pointing to the screen.

Marvin wandered over and peered at the internal job advert on the monitor.

'Source Development Unit,' he murmured. 'Nope. Never heard of it.' He sat back down at his desk, a mountain of unnecessary paperwork threatening to engulf him.

I scanned the requirements for the job and gleefully noticed that the senior officer in charge of the unit had been a detective sergeant in my office when I was at West End Central. He was a very well-respected officer, and rightly so, in the field of covert policing. I knew it was something to do with informants ('source' is essentially a polite name for a snout), and my recent dealings with Harry up north had ignited a spark of interest. I made a call and arranged to go and see the senior officer at the Yard.

The Source Development Unit was part of the same SO10 covert operations department as the Undercover Unit. I was eager to find out more about what they did, as the advert was evidently purposely vague. Later that week, I went to see the DCI as arranged, in his small but comfortable office at the Yard. He greeted me eagerly and said he would love me to work on the SDU.

'Christian, glad you could come, mate. I remember when you used to tear around Soho, nicking everyone, you and that other guy . . . Adrian?' he said.

'Yes, guv. Back in the day!' I replied wistfully.

Buoyed by the fact that such a well-thought-of and well-connected senior officer remembered my work ethic from so many years ago, I asked him what the job was all about.

He explained that it was a new unit focused on recruiting informants. The methods used by the unit were many. Suffice to say that it would be utterly foolhardy to go into them in any depth, but once the unit had identified a potential informant great lengths would be taken to communicate with that person, make an initial approach to them and cultivate them as a source. The unit took great pride in being thorough and diligent, and putting the safety of any potential informant first.

It sounded like a great gig, and definitely something I wanted to get involved in.

'It sounds great, boss,' I said to the DCI.

'Good. Make sure you apply,' he replied. This was Met Police-speak for, 'If you want the job, it's yours.'

'Come and meet the team.' He stood up and led me into the office next door, which was substantially bigger than his.

I was introduced to Angus, a wily detective sergeant on the brink of retirement. I was subsequently to find out that he was probably the wisest colleague I ever worked with, full of excellent advice and opinions based upon years of experience in dealing with thick-headed bosses, irreverent peers and idiotic subordinates. If there is one person whose advice I wish I had heeded, it is him.

Angus looked me up and down, and was not impressed. He was clean-cut and old-school, highly organised and assiduous. God only knows what he thought of me, in a crumpled shirt, with tattoos and shoulder-length hair. Angus was the sort of man who shaved daily and had his hair cut weekly. He shook my hand, nearly breaking the fingers.

The DCI summarised my CV, and when he told Angus I was a UCO, Angus raised his eyes to heaven. 'Not another Miami Vice wannabe,' he said, only half-joking. I smirked and he asked his oft-repeated question, 'Have you got the helicopter or the Lamborghini parked outside?'

Smiling, I said, 'I take it you don't get on with SO10?'

'You mean the Dream Factory?' asked Angus. 'They're a bunch of wannabe gangsters.'

I laughed with him. I could see where he was coming from.

Angus introduced me to the rest of the team and explained a little more about the work they did. I would have to go on several training courses before joining the unit properly and would need to be security vetted to the highest level.

'It sounds like an interesting job,' I said to Angus.

'It's interesting, yes,' he said, 'but if you've never recruited or handled informants before, it's a steep learning curve. Never trust a snout. That's my golden rule.'

'Oh, OK,' I said. 'I'll remember that.'

I said my goodbyes (Angus breaking my fingers a second time with his vice-like handshake) and got back to my office at Marylebone nick.

A few days later the application form, which I had diligently filled out as soon as I returned from my visit to the SDU, was unceremoniously chucked on my desk by Marvin.

'The DI won't sign it,' he said. 'He won't let you go. We're short of DCs.'

'What? You are fucking joking?' I said. 'This opportunity only comes up every now and then. What's he playing at?'

'He's made his mind up, mate,' said Marvin. 'Sorry.'

Fuming, and convinced this was some sort of spiteful managerial vengeance for my refusal to comply with the daily statistic-gathering exercise, I thought, 'OK, he wants to fuck about, does he?'

I made phone calls to several senior officers, all of whom I had worked with at some point or other. I explained my predicament to each one of them. They had substantial influence and contacts in the Met, and I was reassured when, several hours later, Marvin called me on my mobile.

'Mate, you can take that application directly to HR yourself,' he said. 'It's fine, the guvnor has authorised it now.'

Grinning, I scooped up the orange docket with the application form inside and delivered it by hand later that day. Once again, I'd proved that rule in the Met: 'It's not what you know, it's who you know.'

My new day job was to recruit, manage and cultivate informants to help combat high-level criminality – the upper echelons of organised crime in London. The idea was that my unit would be asked to do this by other departments. So, for example, the Central Task Force was a specialist team that dealt with organised crime. They used wiretaps and had a surveillance capacity, but if they were trying to target a particular group or person and might not have had success by normal means, they would come to us with the details of the gang and specify the problem. On paper, it was fantastic, and for the first year it was excellent.

There were only six of us in the unit, but for our size we did remarkably well. I had a great deal of success on that unit and felt I was well regarded. We recruited some useful informants, some so sensitive I wouldn't dream of mentioning them here. We were particularly adept at recruiting informants able to infiltrate Eastern European organised crime.

I found the work exciting and, for the most part, extremely interesting. We got involved in some incredible long-term operations. A lot of the recruitment and cultivation process was painstaking. The reward, for me, however, was the opportunity to meet some pretty brave individuals from the upper echelons of criminality. Brave because they would finally make that life-changing decision to assist the authorities and provide information on some of the most badass criminals in the country.

Think of some stereotypical movie criminals and, believe me, they exist in reality. From broken-nosed bouncers to elegantly coiffed, camp car showroom owners, from Savile Row besuited accountants to scrawny, estate-dwelling hood rats, we surveilled, approached, cultivated and recruited them all.

Everything we did revolved around the safety and security of our potential sources. This was the main reason for our covert cover stories and identities. The slightest sniff of anything wrong and any meets would be abandoned. We were constantly aware, always conducting sophisticated and complex anti- and counter-surveillance drills, to the extent where it almost became second nature. Even now, I have a pretty keen sense of environmental awareness.

I worked with a fantastic team of professionals, led by the robust Angus. He maintained delightfully handwritten operational ledgers, his fountain-pen copperplate script gracing all of the unit's reports back to the management. He was, rightly so, pernickety about solid and timely paperwork and admin. I think that, despite his initial misgivings about me, he was in the end proud of my victories in recruiting some difficult individuals.

The trouble was we eventually became victims of our own success. We would spend months cultivating a contact to the point where they would be a reliable snout. At that stage, we would hand them over to a source unit to handle them from there. Sometimes I had people in tears because I had to break it to them that our relationship was now over and they'd be dealing with someone else. On other occasions, people phoned me up and requested that I be their handler. I couldn't do that. I had enough on my plate.

For each potential snout, I had a different telephone number, so I was running several mobile phones at the same time. Only once the source was recruited would I ditch the SIM card. At one stage, I was juggling nearly a dozen contacts – and that meant a dozen aliases for me. I had so many mobiles on my desk I'd forget which one was mine. Add to this the mobiles and identities I was running for the undercover jobs, and I started to lose track of who I was supposed to be to each contact.

For my source development identity, I had a driving licence, a passport and a National Insurance card. For my undercover identity, I had those plus bank cards. These were all created in collusion with the relevant departments inside these institutions, so, for example, the DVLA has a department tasked with assisting the police with fake driving licences. With the passports, you could travel abroad and use them. I only travelled abroad once – to a far-off former Soviet enclave to meet some people I might be working with, some foreign undercover officers – but effectively I entered the country illegally. The authorities never knew who we were. When people enter the UK, we ask for real identities, but no one seems to consider it when we go abroad.

When the source unit was going well, it was one of the jobs I enjoyed the most. The role tested my communication skills to the max. It was covert policing, but not in a James Bond type of way. The use of informants was an old-fashioned form of law enforcement, written about in *The Art of War*, the ancient Chinese text on military strategy. In this revered text, Sun Tzu questioned whether military leaders who committed hundreds of thousands of men, marching them great distances at great cost to the state, were true leaders of men. He said that what enabled wise men to achieve things beyond the reach of ordinary men was 'foreknowledge' and stated that knowledge of the enemy's thinking could be obtained only from other men. He went on to list five types of spies, from local operatives to converted sources. The language might have changed over the centuries, but the philosophy remained the same. Any operation will be greatly enhanced by the use of good sources.

It's a world that is tightly regulated. After the antics of the old Flying Squad in the 1970s, when it was one of the most easily corruptible parts of the police and there were claims of bent detectives using informants for their own ends, misusing the intelligence and sometimes even skimming off the reward money for themselves, it has been cleaned up. During my time, there continued to be financial rewards for informants depending on the information they provided – at one stage it was revealed that £2.2 million was paid by the Met to sources in a single year – but only in very few cases did people receive salaries. For instance, we had one source who passed on information that a criminal had guns in their possession. Firearms were a huge deal for the Met. The premises were raided, the guns recovered the same day and removed from the street, and the informant received £8,000 for his trouble.

Despite my enthusiasm for the job, because I was working for the part-time index on top of the day job, something had to give – and inevitably it was me. I would be constantly berated anyway by Angus for concentrating too much on undercover work and not enough on the SDU jobs. I started working on a job involving foreign undercover officers coming over to work in London. It was a big operation targeting organised crime. As I spoke Russian, it was my job to sort out the logistics for and liaise with our overseas visitors.

While doing all this, I made a major mistake. I couldn't believe it. Inadvertently, I'd linked a whole host of police activity to an address where foreign undercover officers were staying. I faced a dilemma. Do I tell SO10 what I've done and accept that I'm going to get the bollocking of a lifetime? It's probably what I should have done, but it's impossible to describe the fear in which you hold that office when you work for SO10. To admit an error is a weakness. It was the last place on earth where you'd find a culture of 'Don't worry – if you fuck up, come and see me'. No way. Even if someone did say that, you'd think they were lying.

I felt overwhelmed with dismay and fear, having potentially fucked up such a long-term job. I bit my nails to the quick over a period of days, making myself ill with worry. I was anxious that I had put an end to my career with SO10 before it had even got off the ground. While I held my SO10 colleagues in high esteem, usually, I didn't ever feel like I was comfortable enough to admit this silly error. I wouldn't hear the end of it, and my paranoia developed to such an extent that I felt convinced I was going to get the sack.

It was the same thing when I went for my regular psychological assessments. They were obviously billed as a forum to air any issues and discuss any problems. But they were a complete waste of time. Like you'd ever open up and tell the geezer there the truth about how you felt. You went in there thinking, 'If I tell how I'm really feeling, how fucked up I feel, I'll never be able to do any work again.' That attitude was always in the back of my mind. I always felt there would be a black mark against the name of an operative who had dared to admit his weaknesses, his true feelings or any sense of disquiet, that it would be career suicide.

No, it was best, I decided, to keep quiet and pray no one ever became suspicious enough to do their own checks on that property.

Plus, I had bigger things to worry about. For the first time since I'd joined the part-time index, there were vacancies with the full-time undercover unit. My dream of finally joining the 'best of the best' in UK policing was close to becoming a reality.

17

BIG FAT GYPSY HEADACHE

I HAD LEFT. AFTER MANY YEARS OF ARGUING, I WAS NOW on my own. I had left Jane and my two kids. We hadn't been happy together for a long time. Often, I'd had work to go to at all hours, so it hadn't really mattered so much. On the SDU, the hours were a bit more fixed, and now I was a fully fledged UC there would be no more 70- or 80-hour weeks. UC operations were a lot more irregular and infrequent than TP operations, so there was no guarantee of overtime.

It was a relatively easy decision to make. The thing that really worried me was the impact such a huge change would have on my two sons. I knew that we had taught them to be strong-willed and determined, however, and, despite a promise to myself years ago never to do to my kids what my dad did to me, I ended up doing exactly that.

I'd had a fantastic first year on the SDU, but with mounting debts, and the vast changes in my own life, I started to feel, little by little, like I was losing control.

I remember coming in one morning and laying out, on my desk, all the mobile phones I had. The nature of the job was that you needed different phones to speak to different people. A total of 11 mobile phones were spread across my desk. Jesus.

I started to get very behind on my paperwork, and whereas previously I had carefully submitted everything in a timely fashion, I began to accrue receipts for my SDU and UC expenses and just ended up sticking them in a drawer. I became very lazy, overwhelmed with fatigue and having little or no interest in work at all.

I would regularly come in and make comments about my colleagues, sometimes crossing the line between banter and causing offence. I would say that one day I would lose the plot and shoot everyone with a Kalashnikov.

I wanted to do more UC work, despite this. Christ only knows why. I think I maybe began to believe the hype even more, thinking that SO10 was the pinnacle, the elite. That was where I wanted to be. One day I would come to work feeling full of the joys of spring, ready to rock and roll and do a good job; other days I would sullenly sit around, browsing the Internet, and waiting to go home or go for a drink with my mates at 4 p.m. This boredom was only temporarily alleviated by helping out on the occasional informant training course or helping one of the other SDU staff devise a plan for approaching a potential snout.

After some months, I ended up meeting Grace. I knew Grace from years ago. I had role-played on the TP course she had undertaken and she had done some TP work for me when I worked in central London. Although I knew her, I hadn't really met her or spoken to her for a great length of time when we happened across each other at a job function.

We hit it off rather well and began seeing each other. Grace soon became pregnant, which was something of a surprise. I don't think either of us knew how to feel about it initially. It was another time of huge angst. I didn't tell anyone. I think a couple of people in my office thought I was losing it, as I would disappear for hours on end, wandering around the streets near Scotland Yard on the phone to Grace, deciding what to do.

We eventually went for a scan. Both of us were nervous and frightened. The scan told us that there was in fact no baby, that it had died very early into the pregnancy and was extremely tiny. We were told to return in a couple of weeks for another scan to decide how to deal with the minuscule foetus.

Even though we were unsure of our decision about the baby, we were both devastated. It was like being kicked in the face and I couldn't believe that this had happened. We went through a quite profound period of, well, I suppose, bereavement. This event just compounded my issues at work and I lost all interest. I knew that my work rate was starting to get me noticed for all the wrong reasons.

A couple of weeks later, Grace and I went to the hospital. Surrounded by the teenage matriarchs of east London and their chunky-gold-bracelet-wearing babyfathers, we sat in the cold waiting room. Eventually, we were called in, and nothing was said. I assumed some sort of procedural options were going to be explained to us, about aborting the remains of the foetus and suchlike. We had read about it on the Internet and it didn't sound too nice.

The scan operator began spreading the jelly over Grace's tummy. The screen was not visible to us yet, and as she began the scan she looked at us and said, 'OK. Baby's fine.'

'What?' we both said. 'What do you mean?' We were puzzled.

'Baby's fine,' she repeated in her strong East African

accent. 'It's looking very healthy for its age.'

'So it's not dead?' asked Grace.

'We were here to have a scan and talk about dealing with a dead foetus,' I explained.

'Oh, I'm sorry about that. It just says here a routine scan,' she replied nonchalantly.

How's that for a headfuck? A surprise pregnancy, then the baby is dead and now it isn't. Fuck me. I think the potential for joy was totally eliminated at that point by the disjointed manner in which our brains were operating. It was a bizarre sensation of not quite being able to make sense of what was going on.

For the second time in two weeks, we wandered out of a medical institution in a daze. We did come to terms with it, however, and of course were pleased. Neither of us would have chosen an abortion if we'd felt we had any other option, and I certainly have very strong views on a baby's right to life.

The pregnancy would not be easy. It was deemed high risk by the doctors, as they had identified a possible heart problem. This meant extra appointments, more doctors, different hospitals. We tried to steel ourselves for the difficult months ahead.

At work, I still told no one. I was offered a bit-part role on a long-term UC operation, which I grasped happily. But it wouldn't be that easy.

'Angus,' I said. 'It's only two full days a week.'

'No. The Dream Factory can fuck off. You've got enough work on in here,' he said.

I marched up to the SO10 office and spoke to Brian, the DS in charge of the operation that Angus was refusing to let me work on.

'Don't worry, son,' he said. 'I'll speak to the big boss.'

Feeling slightly guilty about having taken such a course of action, especially against Angus, whom I liked and respected immensely, I nipped outside the Yard to have a fag and quell the impulsive thoughts I was having.

In my heart of hearts, I knew that committing to two days a week on a long-term UC job was foolhardy, especially with the new baby on the way. I would often spend hours fretting and worrying about it, something I was never normally prone to doing. I hated having to side with Brian, as I knew he had no time for me, and I disliked what I saw as his testosterone-fuelled posturing. And I really didn't want to let down Angus or my DCI by seemingly leaving them in the lurch. And yet there was this inexplicable SO10 tractor beam, which, despite my true thoughts and best intentions, dragged me slowly away from rational action. Christ knows why I succumbed to it.

Wandering back upstairs, I received a call from a fuming Angus, who grabbed me in the corridor (not literally grabbed me – verbally) and took me into the DCI's office.

'Right, I need to know what's going on, Christian,' he said. 'Your work is slipping and I'm getting phone calls from commanders about releasing you to do undercover work. So what's up?'

'Nothing, Angus,' I replied. 'I'm sorry.'

'Listen,' he said, 'I know you've had a lot of change in your personal life, and I don't mean to pry, but my suggestion to you is you forget the Dream Factory for a while, knuckle down here and sort your personal issues out, OK?'

This was essentially an offer of help and support from the almost retiree. It was the closest anyone in the job ever came to saying to me, 'Stop what you're doing. Sit down. Take stock. Sort your stuff out and we'll support you.' Angus was a lot more astute than he let on. I wish I had seen it like that at the time. Instead, I shrugged it off.

'Look, I'm fine, I'm fine,' I said, still convinced that any admission of 'stress' or 'difficulties' would end my career.

'OK, if you're sure,' said Angus, reluctantly and disbelievingly. 'Well, I don't think you should do it, but we've agreed to let you do two or three days a week on this fucking Dream Factory nonsense over in Romford.'

'Oh, brilliant, thanks!' I said.

'You need to sort yourself out, though, Christian,' he added.

'Yeah, yeah, OK,' I said dismissively, and left the office, bounding upstairs to the SO10 hub. There, I found Brian and Reg, one of the full-time undercover officers. I was to be working with Reg, apparently, on this new job.

We slipped into the small back office, where Reg gave me a rundown of the job. I was to spend some time in a pub (surprisingly enough) in Romford, opposite a gypsy or travellers' site. Reg was already firmly ensconced in the community and had based himself out of another nearby pub. I was to be an employee of the fictitious firm that Reg had set up, with a large warehouse in the area and a company van. I was, however, to specifically concentrate on this pub, which was apparently a hotbed of crime, with travellers making drug and gun deals daily, and the rest of the punters all bang at it as well – a proper den of iniquity. I was to spend at least two days a week there, with at least one overnight stay in Reg's flat.

'OK,' I thought, 'I'll give it a go.' I was slightly annoyed that the SO10 obsession with pubs continued, and because my profile didn't really fit in with a slaggy pub full of Irish travellers. However, I secretly thought that this could be my pass into the inner sanctum of the SO10 full-time unit.

Much to Angus's irritation, I marked two days a week off on our duties noticeboard in the SDU. The next day, I met the DCI in charge of the operation and got my briefing from him. I decided to make it very plain to him that my other half was in the first stages of a difficult pregnancy and I had no intention of spending 24 hours a day on the plot. If I had to go, I would go. I was slightly apprehensive about the response, but he seemed relaxed about my suggestion. This seemed to pose no problem for him, and I set off for my first visit to The Tramshed.

Situated on the periphery of a huge council estate, The Tramshed was essentially a concrete-clad Portakabin. It was difficult, if not impossible, to identify the building as a pub. Rusty grilles covered the tiny windows, and huge steel doors marked the entrances at both ends of the squat rectangle. Directly opposite the pub was a patch of grass, currently home to two bedraggled horses, obviously animals from the travellers' site opposite.

I turned up there for the first time at about midday. Lunchtime. I would have said it was an excellent excuse to visit a pub, but this establishment was not on a road where you would pop in, as a passer-by. It was an estate pub, pure and simple, and anyone 'popping in' would be eyed with some suspicion.

Outside, sitting at the two picnic tables, were an assortment of locals dressed in the latest fashions from Sports Direct – Lonsdale trainers and three-quarter-length Adidas tracksuit bottoms. I had acquired a nice pair of Nike Air Max 90s for this job, but they were slightly too high end. As I walked into the pub, nervous as usual, a young child of about two ran out to its mother, who was sucking on a Mayfair fag. The kid was wearing nothing but a saggy nappy and a replica England shirt, although, I noted, it was nicely complemented by the gold earrings in each lobe. The kid was carrying a packet of salt-and-vinegar crisps and a plastic bottle of Fanta. Breakfast, I supposed.

Into the lions' den. The pub was almost empty inside. A few old boys sat at the bar, and the far side of the pub (which I would soon realise was the travellers' section) hosted several shaven-headed youths talking loudly in thick Irish accents. Nobody stopped and turned to look at me, as I'd expected, and the cheery barmaid cooed across the bar, 'Mornin', luv, what can I get ya?' Uncomfortably switching into my awful mockney accent, I asked for a pint and a ham roll. 'Paul, one 'am roll, please,' she hollered as she pulled my lager into a pint glass.

I sat at the bar, nursing my pint of Stella, reading the newspaper I had bought earlier (*The Sun*, obviously), silently taking in my surroundings and the type of punters therein. After ten minutes or so, Paul, the 70-year-old landlord, plonked a chipped china plate in front of me, upon which was a crusty white roll containing a wedge of ham about half a centimetre thick and a generous amount of butter, which was oozing out of the bread.

''Am roll?' he asked.

'Cheers,' I said, and gingerly bit into it. It was absolutely fucking rancid. The sensation of the wads of cheap butter (I prefer a light dash of low-fat olive-oil spread) and thick chewy ham going down my throat was not one I would wish to experience again. I washed each mouthful down with a generous swig of Stella, almost gagging each time.

That first day, I stayed in the pub until about 6 p.m. I had only had three pints but felt quite pissed. Still, I was a rufty-tufty UC officer and, naturally, I drove home.

Over the next couple of months, I spent hours in The Tramshed, sometimes in the daytime, sometimes in the evening, but never later than nine because I wanted to get home to Grace. I soon got to know the regulars, the bar staff and the landlord. Everyone who was in that pub, especially in the evenings, was a working man. I saw some tiny bits of naughtiness, like people buying DVDs off the Vietnamese guy who arrived every Thursday afternoon, or the odd oik nipping off to the toilet for a line of charlie, or the junkie shoplifter selling bits of make-up he had nicked from the market. It was just run-of-the-mill local-pub goings-on.

After a long time, the DCI asked me what was happening.

'It's just not a criminal pub, guv. Yeah, there are some scrotes in there, but they're not doing anything, and most people in there are working guys, making money for their families.'

'OK, keep at it. There must be something going on,' he said.

I began to get a bit disheartened with it all. Nothing in the pub was out of the ordinary or worth pursuing at all. The travellers, while very rowdy and noisy, didn't cause too many issues, and if there were ever any fights it was amongst themselves. I saw no evidence of shady dealings, whispered conversations or drug dealing.

I started to think to myself, 'What the fuck am I doing in here? This is a pointless exercise. I hate pubs. I hate this part of London.' Each time I went there, I would be driving after four or five pints, pissed in a work car. If I got pulled over, I'd be done. I must have driven while under the influence several times. I would have been instantly dismissed. Part of me didn't give a fuck, though. It was disillusionment. It was a journey of self-destruction.

'If this is what they want me to do,' I reasoned, 'then so be it.' I couldn't generate criminals. They were down on their luck and they were surviving. If a bloke was stealing meat from Tesco to sell in the pub, who was I to pull him in? It wasn't fair on them to be caught in the net because SO10 wanted results from a poor tip in the first place. I couldn't believe I had done my national undercover course for this.

It was shit.

One day, I got a call from Brian at SO10. 'Christian, we need you to spend a whole evening and night over there,' he said. Obviously, the DCI was not happy that I was only spending a few hours at a time in the pub. I said that I only went home in the evening because it wasn't fair on Grace to be left on her own overnight while she was pregnant.

'Yeah, we know that, but you need to spend a bit more time there. Go on Thursday night – it's karaoke night – and I'll send Freddy down there too.'

'Oh God, OK,' I replied.

Freddy, a larger-than-life cockney gangster type, was a very experienced UCO, and very good company. He loved a drink, and I was sure that if anyone could sniff out some crime in the pub it would be him.

Freddy had had some bit roles in this operation already, and we decided that he could be someone for whom I had worked in the past. So, one balmy Thursday evening, we arrived at the pub at about 7 p.m. and the drinking began. From the off, Freddy was his usual self, loud and extroverted. I'm pretty sure he turned some heads. I have to say, I got very merry very quickly. I suspect some underhand drink-spiking was going on, but I'll never be sure! Freddy had me in stitches at the karaoke, and it certainly got him noticed by the regulars.

At one point, Freddy returned from the toilet and whispered, 'I've just been fronted out.'

'What do you mean?' I asked.

'Just been fronted out about being Old Bill,' he said.

'Oh, fuck. Who by?' I said.

'The pikeys,' he said. 'But don't worry, it's fine.'

Probably because of my overindulgence in alcohol, I paid little heed to this ominous turn of events. The night continued until just about midnight. I hadn't really achieved very much, apart from becoming dizzyingly drunk. I could hardly see or stand, and I knew what I had to do.

Staggering through the travellers' side of the pub to the far exit, I careered through the doors and onto the footpath. Bending forward, I resolutely stuffed two fingers down the back of my throat and vomited. I repeated this a couple of times.

Once satisfied that I was OK, I slowly stood back up, avoiding the puddle of spew between my feet, and wandered back towards the doors of the pub. As I did so, a group of travellers, all of whom I had seen at one point or another in the pub over the last few weeks, were coming out.

'See you, lads,' I said.

One of them slapped me hard on the back, and smiled, 'See you later, sergeant!'

There was a chorus of laughs.

'Yeah,' chimed in another, 'you go back to the station now, officer.'

I realised what they were saying. They were saying I was a cop. I was not a cop – I was Christian Sulyenko. Bravado, fuelled by alcohol, kicked in. 'You fucking what?' I said, getting nose to nose with the biggest traveller in the group. 'You saying I'm Old Bill?'

'Yeah,' he replied, gently shoving me backwards, 'you and your fat mate in there. You're both dirty fucking coppers and we think you should fuck off.'

Thanks to the alcohol, I felt little anxiety. 'What the fuck are you talking about, you cunt?' I screamed. 'Fucking coppers? You're taking the fucking piss!'

I noticed Paul, the landlord, and Freddy coming outside.

Freddy joined in what essentially became a slanging match, with all of us shouting abuse. I saw a few of the lads had their fists clenched, while some had picked up rocks from the nearby patch of land.

'Listen, you bastards, if you don't want to get your heads kicked in, you better fuck off now,' said the ringleader.

'I ain't fucking off nowhere!' shouted Freddy as the group began advancing on us.

Paul the landlord said, 'Get the fuck inside now, you two.' He grabbed my arm.

'Cunts!' shouted Freddy as Paul bundled us inside and hurriedly bolted the steel security door.

The travellers began hammering on the door, kicking and shouting. It was fairly terrifying, now I recall it. Freddy's reaction, and mine, was solely down to alcohol, I reckon.

'Stay here, lads,' said Paul.

The hammering and shouting died down after some minutes, and Paul had a swift peek through the window. 'They've all gone, boys. Dirty pikey cunts, always causing trouble,' he said.

'Fuck knows what that was all about,' I said. 'Fucking Old Bill? Where the fuck did they get that from?'

'Aw, don't worry about it,' said Paul. 'It's just cos they don't know you, that's all.' I could see some suspicion in his eyes.

Still not sober, Freddy and I decided to walk back to the

covert flat nearby. This meant walking past the travellers' site.

'Cheers, Paul,' I said. 'Thanks for getting us out of that.'

'That's OK,' he said. 'You lads have a safe night.'

Freddy and I walked out into the night, and as soon as we got about 20 yards away from the pub, we looked at each other and cracked up laughing. We staggered back to the flat, reliving the incident, already turning it into a tall tale, a legendary occasion, for consumption back at SO10. As we wobbled past the traveller site, we both shouted out 'Wankers!' and ran off, like a couple of kids.

We crashed out at the flat and I woke early. My head was spinning, and it was only then that I realised the severity of the situation. It could have quite easily turned pear-shaped and Freddy and I could have ended up in hospital, or worse.

You would have thought, after such a debacle, that somebody would have spoken to us about what went on. The opposite was the case. I didn't speak to anyone about it. I never heard from the cover officer or the team again. No one said, 'You fucked that up. You're off the job.' Nobody said anything. It went from being a significant priority – a hotbed of criminality that had to be smashed – to nothing. As far as I was aware, the job carried on without my section.

My head throbbed with conflicting emotions. I was glad to be off the case; it had driven me to despair. But the manner in which my involvement stopped frustrated me. For months, I'd visited the pub and had never been challenged about whether I was a copper. Then, when they sent reinforcements, it took less than a night. Freddy and I were chalk and cheese, but things like that were never considered by SO10, it seemed to me.

I started to wonder whether I'd made a terrible mistake by placing so much faith in the Undercover Unit. It seemed to me now that it was anything but elite. What lay in store for me next, I wondered?

18
SUICIDAL

HERE WE GO AGAIN. I COULD FEEL IT COMING. THERE'S a strange sense of calm when you know things are about to spiral out of control.

I think the perception is that it's the big things that tip you over the edge. Often, though, it's the most inconsequential crap that does it. Never would I have thought that Grace having a go at me for smoking again would be the thing that pushed me into this dark place. But that was the only thing I could put my finger on. She only had my health at heart, yet to me I felt like a smackhead failing to convince her I was clean.

Sounds crazy, but it was enough to light the touchpaper. Somehow, if I wasn't good enough in her eyes, then I was worth nothing. She was all I had. Without her, there was nothing left worth living for.

Anyone on the outside looking in might have thought being set upon by a dozen marauding gypsies might have been the tipping point. The reality, though, was that I relished those fuckers coming at me. At least in that moment I could see the problem in front of me, could see the bricks and stones they'd use to smash my face in. Even the bollocking that should have followed that job I could have handled. Far worse was the lack of response. That was the killer: not knowing what they were thinking or what they were planning for punishment. It was doing my nut in.

The dull headache I experienced with every stressful job was now a constant presence, an incessant throbbing no paracetamol could soothe. Yet, despite this, what I craved was to be in the firing line again. At least then I'd be in the thick of it, be a copper again. I needed something to take my mind off this creeping death.

I had a couple of days' leave until I next reported for duty and already I could feel the hiatus destroying me. I opened my pants drawer and stared once again at the pile of crumpled receipts. It was like they were taunting me, a constant reminder of my uselessness. I had a sense that this untidy mess of paper would eventually be the thing that did me in, but I still couldn't bring myself to tackle it. It was absolutely ridiculous. What did they say we were? The best of the best? The SAS of the police? It was about as far from 'elite' as you can get. Imagine being told you are part of the SAS, and the reality is you are actually a clerk in the Adjutant General's Corps.

Now, one of the so-called elite was being brought to his knees by paperwork. I could almost see the headlines now: 'Top cop driven to suicide by pen pushers'. It would have been laughable if it hadn't been so damned scary.

It wasn't just the receipts, of course. My evidential notebooks were now so severely lacking in detail sometimes they didn't even contain actual evidence. I thought of the long series of bad decisions I had behind me – the main one being doing the fucking undercover course in the first place. What had happened to me? Not that long ago I was a shit-hot cop. Now I was just shit.

The perverse thing was that I wanted my dwindling work ethic to attract the attention of my colleagues at Scotland Yard. I wanted someone to take notice of how fucked up I was. But there was nothing. No one to talk to. No one seemed remotely bothered about what was happening to me. I wanted to go to the SO10 office and scream: 'I HAVEN'T SUBMITTED ANY EXPENSES FOR MONTHS, YOU IDIOTS! PLEASE CAN YOU FUCKING HELP ME?'

I was now on the floor of the lounge, tears streaming down my face, gulping huge lungfuls of air between sobs. Then, as my throat dried up, I could smell my breath, smell my stench. I hadn't showered, shaved or brushed my teeth. I repulsed myself.

The tears kept coming. I'd had enough. Something had to give. I had to end this – end everything. No more forgetting who I was when I left the house in the morning, no more SO10 thinking I was a useless prick, no more fretting over lapsed paperwork, no more disappointing Grace with my pathetic behaviour. I'm going mad, I thought. I must be to be even contemplating this. But if I know I'm going mad, am I actually mad?

Eventually, I calmed down and stood up. I felt strangely detached, almost giddy. Suddenly things were quite clear. I could see a solution.

I was going to kill myself. Just thinking about it was calming me down, making things clearer. A plan formed in my head, as straightforward, it seemed, as any operation.

The next few hours were spent in an almost dreamlike state. I became quite matter-of-fact and almost organised about everything. I had a shower. There was a good reason for this. I didn't want my body found in an unclean state or with dirty pants. That wouldn't be fair, I thought.

I packed a small hold-all with all my undercover documents. Three passports, three driver's licences and several bank and credit cards. I also grabbed the multitude of receipts and cash and expenses forms from my pants drawer. I think I shoved some clothes in the bag too, just for appearances' sake.

My plan seemed quite simple. I was going to travel to Victoria, take a train to Dover and then walk onto the cross-Channel ferry using one of my fake passports. Once aboard, I'd ceremoniously toss all of my SO10 documents and all the other shitty paperwork I had accrued into the Channel. Then I would throw myself in. From my marine police training, I knew I would succumb very swiftly to the cold water, be rendered unconscious and then peacefully drown.

I got my notepad and envelopes from the car. I wrote very short notes to my loved ones, including one to my unborn son that said, 'If you are anything like your mum, you will be perfect.'

My longest letter was to the commissioner, blaming the Met Police for pushing me to this point. In this, I enclosed my real warrant card.

In all there were seven letters, which I arranged, clearly marked, on my kitchen sideboard.

I removed the battery from my Blackberry and left it, discarded, in my lounge, along with the keys to the Jag that I had left parked outside my house in a resident's bay. Perhaps I was secretly hoping that the car would get a ticket or get checked on the police computer, alerting SO10 to a possible problem. Maybe it was a last cry for help.

I gathered my stuff together and shut the front door. Only when I started walking did the enormity of what I was doing hit me. I shakily made my way to the Tube station around the corner. Sporadically, I wept, my head shaking. On the platform, I sat, head in hands, shaking uncontrollably.

There, I had a moment of realisation. What the fuck are you doing? Go home. Maybe I wasn't going mad. I walked home, but by the time I reached the flat those thoughts had gone, replaced by darker ones once more.

I grabbed my Blackberry, replaced the battery and again strode out of the flat to the station, more purpose in my steps this time. As if in a trance, I made it to Victoria. I bought a Starbucks latte. 'Hey, you only commit suicide once,' I thought.

I bought a one-way ticket to Dover and sat sipping my coffee by the busy bus station. Random thoughts filtered into my head as I sat there. I kept checking my phone, hoping for some message or call that would change my mind. None came.

I knew if I got on the Dover train there would pretty much be no turning back. I was thinking about getting through the security check at the port. What if they searched my bag and found different passports? What would I do?

I was close to the Yard. Surely someone I knew would pass, see me and stop for a chat. I'd take that as a sign not to go through with this.

My thoughts turned to the notes I had left, and I remembered my partner had door keys for my flat. I imagined the awful scene when she arrived there and all the frightening stuff that would then happen – the big search, the investigation. In her state, that was the last thing she needed.

I needed affirmation. I needed counselling. I called my mate Justin. He'd know what to say. He'd get it straight away and convince me not to go through with this. His number rang. Come on, pick up. If this was a sign, it was pointing only one way at the moment.

I then thought again of my unborn son.

It was like a light flickering in the darkest reaches of my mind. Prompted into action, I headed back into the station, but instead of aiming for the train to Dover, I made for the Underground. My panic now was to get home before Grace found the notes. The journey back took forever. I started to sweat. Fuck, what if she found the notes. It would all kick off then. Then I remembered the car. What if it got flagged up? I'd really be in the shit. Only moments before I'd been praying those scenarios would unfold; now I was desperate for anything to stop that chain of events happening.

I got home and was relieved to see a ticket-less Jaguar. When I got inside the flat, I saw the farewell letters untouched. I retrieved my warrant card, screwed them all up and put them in the bin. For good measure, I emptied it into the wheelie bin outside.

I sat down in the empty flat once more. Nothing had changed. None of my problems, stresses or thoughts had gone away. I didn't feel any better. I didn't feel any worse. I still felt awful, and still wanted to weep constantly, and still had a huge headache, and still felt nauseous.

But then, in a rare moment of clarity, I made a call to the SO10 administrator and asked for a self-referred appointment to see the psychologist. Hopefully, he'd determine how fucked up I was.

For the moment, however, I had to focus on work. Another day in the office loomed.

19
GOING FULL-TIME

'YOU GOT YOUR CREDIT CARD ON YOU?' THE DS SLURRED drunkenly.

'Er, yeah,' I said. 'Why?'

'You're paying, son,' he said, laughing.

'Yeah, Sulyenko,' scoffed another DS. 'It's your round!'

And so I picked up the tab for a lovely Chinese meal for me and a few other UC officers, some from overseas who were being 'entertained'. The evening had started as a quick social, a beer or two with our comrades from abroad. I would be working with them in the future, on operations in west London – we both spoke a common language – and I was meeting them for the first time.

Of course, being UCs, we had our false identities with us and maintained a semblance of covertness. However, this quickly descended (as it always does) into farce, with loud conversations about undercover jobs past and present, and who'd bought the biggest parcel of gear or the most guns. The usual dick-swinging contest. I had nothing to compare (operationally, I mean!) so kept schtum.

We had eventually repaired to a nearby Chinese restaurant. I actually wanted to go home, but I stuck to the etiquette of this situation: don't fucking leave until the end.

Even in the fragile state I was in, I wanted to be part of it. I don't know why, but I still foolishly yearned to be one of the big boys – the full-timers. I had done bits and bobs, and wanted to be permanently undercover – those guys really were the dog's bollocks. My mind filtered out my apprehension and worry about the baby, about Grace, about my lack of work ethic, and the fact that I had been going to top myself a few weeks ago. Oh no, that didn't even come into it. I wanted to reach the pinnacle!

Yet, despite these idiotic yearnings, I knew in my heart of hearts that I wouldn't be able to do it. I wouldn't be able to commit to the hours and dedication. And, really, I thought that most of the people at SO10 were a bit up themselves. I got especially angered when they would tell their stories of jobs gone by. I felt that none of them would cut it as a crackhead or smackhead, which I still considered to be the real front line and the more dangerous type of work.

One of the officers present at this informal shindig whispered conspiratorially to me that there would be some vacancies on the full-time unit soon. I took this as some sort of nod, a tacit agreement that I could apply and succeed. This pleased me no end.

Slightly uncomfortable about accruing yet another expense on my covert credit card, knowing that the receipt would soon gather dust like the rest, I staggered out of the restaurant with everyone else. Thank fuck, I could go home now.

Some days later, I got a call from one of the DSs in the SO10 office informing me that applications were indeed open for the full-time unit.

It was utterly apparent to my colleagues in the SDU that

I had other things on my mind. I would spend hours away from the office, smoking furiously, pacing up and down outside New Scotland Yard, just generally worrying. I had made no effort in the latest batch of operations to identify or recruit any informants, and the initial glow of success that had accompanied my first year on the SDU had faded fast.

The DCI who recruited me had lost all faith in me, especially after my insistence on doing the gypsy job, and Angus merely castigated me constantly for wanting to be part of the 'Dream Factory'. Although he'd sat me down and, in the manner of a wise yogi, told me to forget SO10 and concentrate on sorting my personal life out, getting on top of things and then cracking on with the SDU, I'd dismissed him as a rambling fool on the brink of retirement who didn't know what he was on about. I sincerely wish I had taken his advice. In retrospect, I let a lot of good people down, but I just felt constantly deflated, with no sense of purpose.

I thought getting on the full-time unit would be the kick up the arse I needed.

'No way,' said the DCI. 'You signed up for the SDU for two years.'

'I know, guv,' I said, 'but it's an opportunity that doesn't come along very often. You know how they work, boss. If you don't take it when it's offered, then you'll never be offered it again.'

'And where does it say that?' he asked. 'Tell me and I'll go straight to the commander now.'

'Well, it's just one of those unwritten things, guv,' I said.

'Well, bollocks. You're not going.' With that, he turned away in his chair.

I opened the door to find Jimmy and Sergei, two of my

SDU colleagues, bent double at the door, having been listening in. Sergei grinned at me and we scurried back into our office.

'Fucking hell, son,' he said, 'the guvnor don't want you to go, does he?'

'Er, no, mate,' I said, 'seems not.'

Why I would have wanted to create more of a stir, I don't know, but I stormed up to the SO10 office. Grabbing the guvnor, I explained that my DCI wouldn't let me go. He merely said, 'OK, OK, leave it with me.'

I wandered out of the office. My head was a complete mess, to be honest. Grace continued to have difficulties with her pregnancy. I still hadn't told anyone at work yet, and we had gone through a complete nightmare at the various hospital appointments we had attended. The baby might be poorly, and the stresses were evident. I knew that going to the SO10 office would mean that senior officers would get involved and that this would put the backs of Angus and the DCI up.

I was, it seemed, utterly past caring, though. I continued to have an awful attitude towards my colleagues, still spending little time doing real work. I maintained a ridiculous level of lethargy, and really all I could think about were the huge changes that were happening in my life. I really didn't have any idea whatsoever how I would be affected by it all. Still, I managed to keep a brave face on it.

All of my colleagues knew I had gone through a break-up, but none of them really pried. I think they assumed it was a typical midlife crisis. I didn't. I had 100 per cent faith, and still do, that it was the correct course to take.

I began to lose contact with other colleagues I had previously worked with, ignoring their calls and emails. I became very withdrawn at home and would often stay in bed all day or lounge around not doing much. Often I would inexplicably burst into tears, and I frequently felt that my head would explode with the pressure of the thoughts rushing through it.

I began to see my inability to sort out my expenses as a nemesis, to the point that I would feel sick just thinking about it and would simply ignore it. In retrospect, it's utterly ridiculous. I only had to fill out some forms, for fuck's sake. The maelstrom of bizarre thoughts I would have focused all my anxieties on these expenses. It was, I assume, a way of keeping my worries, nerves and, dare I say it, depression, under wraps, secret and concealed from the world.

I knew from the symptoms I was suffering that I needed help. Still, though, I didn't ask for it. Although I had asked for an appointment with the psychologist, I didn't push to speed the process up and I still feared that if I said I felt a bit doolally I could wave adieu to any thoughts of going full-time. Had I been thinking sensibly, I would never have considered it. And, really, SO10 should never have considered me for the full-time job.

A few days after my indignant exit from the DCI's office, he called me in.

'Right. The commander has spoken. You start upstairs on Monday,' he said, without an ounce of pleasure.

I grinned. 'Wow, nice one. Thanks, boss,' I said, and made an impassioned, apologetic speech about messing him about.

I so wish I had listened to Angus. The feeling that I let him and the DCI down still haunts me. They were both excellent cops, proper cops, and very good at their jobs. I should have stuck with them.

These contrary feelings were whizzing round my head,

but still I pushed forward, bouncing into the SDU office, announcing my impending departure.

'Fuck,' said Sergei. 'Someone must have pulled some strings, eh?'

'I assume so,' I said, smiling.

I felt on top of the world. I had made it into the elite, the pinnacle of any covert cop's career. And yet, at the same time, I felt terribly unfulfilled. It was stupid. Even though I was elated that I had finally made it, I knew that I wouldn't be able to commit to the full-time undercover remit.

Not many people know that the SO10 full-time unit exists, but it is the elite in British policing when it comes to undercover work. It really is the dog's bananas. You've made it if you get on there. The operations can last between a year and ten years and involve living in a particular area twenty-four hours a day, seven days a week. You might have a shop, a business or even a 'real' job. How on earth did I think I could commit to this? 'Ah, it'll be all right,' I thought. 'They'll understand.'

Such operations have to be justified at all times. They involve an extreme level of intrusion into people's lives and there is this huge element, of course, of deception.

The role Mark Kennedy played in infiltrating a group of environmental protesters is a prime example of a long-term infiltration. Long after I encountered him, Mark spent seven years infiltrating green activists while working for the National Public Order Intelligence Unit (NPOIU), a secretive operation that compiles information on activists and extremists. He adopted the fake identity Mark Stone – complete with passport and driving licence – in 2003 and, sporting long hair, piercings and tattoos, pretended to be a professional climber to infiltrate groups protesting against climate change. During his time undercover, he gained access to dozens of groups, travelled to some 22 countries and played a front-line role in some of the biggest demonstrations in the UK, including the G20 protests in London.

However, his role – and the actions of the unit he reported to – was called into question in 2011 after a trial of six activists accused of conspiring to break into Ratcliffe-on-Soar coal-fired power station in Nottinghamshire collapsed. Prosecutors had not made known to the defence teams that Kennedy was an undercover policemen. In the furore that followed, he was accused by one of the defendants of being an agent provocateur, saying that, rather than being a bystander, he had been in the thick of the action. Although Mark, whom I remembered as a stand-up guy and a great policeman, apologised for his actions, he insisted that his superiors were kept informed of his activities at all times. The case raised questions about the role of the undercover police officer and also drew focus onto the secretive NPOIU, which in 2010 was reported to have a budget of £5.7 million and employ some 60 to 70 officers.

Sometimes I thought the reasoning behind running infiltration jobs was weak, to say the least. Exactly as test purchase jobs were justified by linking them to current crime trends, the same applied to these much more expensive and personnel-intensive undercover operations.

Each operation was shrouded in secrecy, so much so that, generally, on the full-time unit, you wouldn't even know what the other UC officers were up to. As well as committing to a full-time operation, you would be expected to undertake bit parts in other, shorter-term jobs, and to maintain your legend-building in the area of London you had been posted to, where you were allocated a rented flat.

However, despite any qualms or worries, I was excited and privileged to enter into this hallowed world. On my first day, I set about arranging my new, covert rented flat. I assumed that I had been recruited in anticipation of a long-term operation. I wondered what it could be and imagined anything from infiltrating a drug gang to exposing an international group of arms dealers.

After longing to join the ranks of the full-time unit for so long, when it happened it was something of an anticlimax. I actually found myself, for the first few weeks, kicking my heels and waiting to be told what to do. I was often told to go legend-building or spend some time with some foreign undercover officers who were working in the UK. I found this quite unsettling. At this point, I was almost programmed to go to work in the morning and come home in the evening. The full-time unit was not like this.

I got thoroughly bored and pissed off the first few weeks. This was meant to be the exciting new job I had always dreamed of. The reality was proving itself to be quite different. I didn't let it show, though.

Even when I was being treated like a glorified gofer, I tried to just suck it up and get on with it. I had to go and collect the detective chief superintendent's car, or go and swap a car over at our garaging facility, or drop something off for someone across London – hardly front-line policing. On top of that, I had to sort out all the crap and bullshit that comes with being someone else – paying bills, answering phone calls, replying to emails.

I ached to do something worthwhile. I felt I had lost my mojo and that I needed to get involved in something that would give me back a bit of faith and restore my snuffed out desire to do some good. My 'magic eye' was still there, but I seriously worried that my heart wasn't in it.

20

SNARING EVIL

'AHA, JUST THE MAN FOR THE JOB,' SMILED CARRIE, A brash Northern detective sergeant.

I looked at her quizzically as I entered the hallowed portal.

'You available for a bit of work?'

'Of course,' I replied.

'We've got a paedo job. Come and have a chat a bit later with the boss from SCD5.'

'OK,' I said, with not a little apprehension. SCD5 was the Paedophile Unit. A lot of their sterling work was conducted on the Internet, with officers posing as paedophiles or young kids to ensnare these perverts when they began committing offences. The main thrust of their job was building a relationship with the offenders online.

However, this was a job where I was going to have to engage in real life with a paedophile. In one of his books, Irvine Welsh described child abusers as pure evil. I tended to agree. As far as I was concerned, child abuse was definitely the most heinous act anyone could commit. Often my liberal views were at odds with many rank-and-file police officers, but when it came to paedophiles these were unceremoniously discarded.

Given my shaky mental state, I should have politely declined. Harbouring such entrenched views about perpetrators like these, and with my recent history, this was probably not the job for me. I should have walked away. But I thought I could handle it. How bad could it be? Although I had reservations, overriding these was the feeling that this could potentially be an operation that would earn me much needed kudos amongst the SO10 clique.

Certainly there wouldn't be many volunteers to do this job. It was not glamorous, there was no flash car or expensive penthouse attached to it, and there would be no talk of 'shooters', 'powder' or 'slaughters'. It definitely wasn't a job for the posse of south-east London gangsters some in SO10 imagined themselves to be. Jobs like this made me feel superior in a way, as I knew most undercover cops wouldn't want to do it, ostensibly because it wasn't sexy but really because they would find it distasteful; despite their bravado and tales of derring-do, they actually wouldn't have the bollocks to do it.

So, with trepidation, I met a couple of guys from the Paedophile Unit. With Carrie there, they gave me a brief rundown of the job and what they wanted me to do. In a nutshell, an SCD5 officer had posed online as a guy who was willing to 'pimp out' his two kids for sexual abuse to a suspected paedophile known as Tony. I was to be Martin, the name the officer had used online. I was shown the chat logs from their online sessions and given a crash course in how these filthy bastards behaved and what sort of language they used. I was advised to start with something innocuous like: 'Isn't it nice when your little girl sits on your lap?' I could feel my stomach churning.

Just by reading the chat, I could see it was sickening stuff and, although the chat logs contained nothing explicit or overly sexual, the undercurrent of the conversations was severely disturbing.

The officers at SCD5 who do this online stuff day in, day out are true heroes, having to soak up this evil and morally decrepit mess and then go home to their families. Unsurprisingly, these officers have an extensive psychological support network, with almost immediate access to shrinks and Occupational Health staff, as well as complete and utter understanding from their superiors. No one would dare to dismiss you out of hand or whisper behind your back if you mentioned getting 'stressed out' at the Paedophile Unit.

'So,' I said to the SCD5 boss, 'you want me to call this bloke, Tony, and try and arrange to meet up so he can have sex with my kids? Is that right?'

'Yes please, Chris,' said the guvnor. 'You OK with this?'

This was a question asked of me constantly throughout the day and the subsequent deployments. It was refreshing to know that my welfare was taken quite seriously. But, still succumbing to the SO10 macho ideal, I suppressed all the uncomfortable thoughts in my head and the nauseous feeling in the pit of my stomach. Spurred on solely by the thought that I would be helping to stop this shitbag sexually assaulting kids, I said, 'Yep, boss. I'm fine.'

'When do you want me to do the first call?' I asked, expecting to arrange to come back to the SCD5 office the following week or sometime in the future.

'In about ten minutes, if poss,' replied the guvnor.

'Oh.' The colour drained from my face and I recall visibly gulping. 'OK, no worries.'

I scrabbled round in my 'man bag' (an item deemed de

rigueur for SO10 UCs and never frowned upon, despite its supposed effeminacy), grabbing my device for recording phone calls (nothing more exotic than a Dictaphone, actually). I was sorted out with an unregistered mobile and I read through the chat logs again, preparing myself for the call.

The general consensus amongst the SCD5 team was that Tony would initially be suspicious, would ask lots of questions and then perhaps arrange to speak to me again on the phone. If we were very lucky, he would agree to meet up. That was all we were expecting: a ten-minute phone call at most.

And indeed that was all, mentally, I prepared myself for. The high-pressure situation meant that my doomed and twisted mind was focusing solely on the matter at hand – no thoughts of suicide or worry were with me now. I could concentrate on nothing but the job. A bizarre paradox – stress curing stress. I think it was to do with the nature of the work. I felt cracking this job was so important, morally and legally, that I gave it all I was worth. Deep down, I thought of the good karma I would get, nailing a paedophile.

So, locked in an anonymous office at SCD5 (phones off the hook, no tannoy speaker, no police radios, etc.), I hooked up the recorder, dialled Tony's number and waited.

After only a couple of rings, he picked up.

'Hello?'

'Hello, Tony, it's Martin, from the website.'

'Oh, hello, mate . . . hold on . . . how are you?'

He sounded amiable enough, and in the brief early exchanges came across like any normal human being. The small talk only lasted a few seconds, however.

Sooner than I was ready for, he got round to the subject

of kids and 'being naked'. Still, to someone who didn't know the circumstances, the conversation could have passed for almost innocent initially. I knew, though, that there was always this awful, malevolent undercurrent.

I made a comment about how nice it was when the kids got out of the bath, or something similar – my intention being to get him to speak about the depraved activities he got up to. My God, talk about lighting the blue touchpaper.

Suddenly, any air of respectability evaporated and Tony launched into detail about the most awful sexual abuse of small children, mainly boys, making it clear he was referring to kids of prepubescent age. It was fucking sick stuff. I wouldn't ever repeat any of it verbatim in print, as I don't want to be party to some sick paedo-porn. (In days gone by, statements by rape and abuse victims used to be sold on in prisons and the like for titillation purposes.) For the next 40 minutes, the guy wouldn't stop talking. He went on and on.

I should have been thinking, 'Brilliant. He's talking about fucking small kids. He is admitting abusing his own kids. He's talking about grooming kids in young families at campsites in Europe. He is fucked. He is going to prison.'

Instead, I was feeling physically sick. I had to enthuse about his conversation, agree with him, say that it was turning me on and that I was getting hard, that I was so aroused I wanted to have a wank. And seriously, with every word I uttered, I could literally feel bile rising.

I knew I was just playing a role, but it was as if his words (and my responses, which were required to maintain my cover) were infecting me somehow. I felt diseased. All I wanted to do was to scream, 'You fucking sick CUNT,' and slam the phone down.

Ever the pro, however, I continued until, no longer able to stand it, I pretended that a 'colleague' was now present and I had to go. I ended the call ridiculously swiftly and took deep breaths. I gave a slurred summary of the call for the benefit of the recorder, which was still active, and in fact I apologised on the recording, stating that I actually felt physically sick.

I gathered myself together and swayed out into the main SCD5 office. Later I was told by one of the SCD5 sergeants that I was white as a sheet.

'So, what happened?' asked the DI.

I blurted out a big, emotional summary. I told him what had been said, and they were ecstatic. It was all good evidence. SCD5 being what it is, I was immediately offered counselling. They asked if I was OK to go on. And, being SO10, I shunned the offer of counselling, almost laughingly. The big bad UC from SO10 who couldn't handle a dirty fucking paedo? No way.

I let Carrie know about the call. She was happy. When I saw her a couple of days later at the SCD10 office, she asked me, sotto voce (there were some shaven-headed SO10 hard nuts in the office), if I wanted to see Occupational Health. She had listened to the recording of the call and wanted to make sure I was OK. That was the only offer of psychological help I ever got from anyone at SO10, and it came from a lovely lady who, because of the nature of the office, had to ask me in a manner as if she was discussing the best way to make Jamaican jerk chicken at a National Front rally.

Of course, I refused the offer. Again.

Believing I was fit to continue, I went on to make other calls to this filthbag Tony. Twice I called him from my home – or rather while sitting outside in my car. On one occasion, I was sitting in the car on the phone to him, pretending to agree with him about the best age to anally rape young boys, when my partner's parents tapped on the window. They had arrived for an unexpected visit. I frantically waved them away. Little did they know I was discussing absolutely evil acts with a paedophile who actually lived in the same town as them.

Eventually, I arranged to meet this bastard at an anonymous café near a west London Tube station. The arrangement – as he understood it – was that he would come to my house and together we would sexually abuse my two children, aged seven and ten. The sick, sick fucker. It angers me even now.

On the morning of the meeting, the SCD5 team briefed me. Then, nervous as hell, I went to the Tube station. I got a text from one of the sergeants saying that Tony (who the team had already identified and put under surveillance) was already at the café. He had been there for more than an hour and had recced the area. This made me more nervous because I was now worrying that he might suspect it was a set-up.

After arriving at the station, I went into the café and saw Tony seated outside. The team had given me a description, but obviously I had to pretend I had no idea who he was.

I called his number and his phone rang. He glanced up at me. This was it. Now the anxiety grew. I remembered some urban myth about how a paedophile could spot another one just by looking at his eyes. Tony looked intently at me. I couldn't hold his gaze for more than a few milliseconds. I wanted to throttle him, choke him to death. He proffered his hand. In a fleeting moment of complete idiocy, I remember thinking, 'Shit, he's convinced!

Does this mean I look like a paedo?' Reluctantly, I shook it, again feeling bile rising. I knew his rough, calloused hand had done untold damage to little kids. I had to tell myself it would all be over shortly.

I forced a smile, and suggested going inside for a quick coffee. Surprisingly, he agreed, and we repaired inside, where the Polish waitress took my order for two cappuccinos. As we sat down at the back of the café, I noted the presence of an SCD5 detective at a nearby table. Other than her, the café was busy with unsuspecting west London yummy mummies.

I saw the SCD5 officer make a call, and I made small talk with Tony, who told me he was looking forward to today and couldn't wait to meet my kids. Grinning, I told him that they couldn't wait to meet him either. He told me he had bought them some presents. I could see he had some Cadbury's Chocolate Buttons in the carrier bag at his feet. I said that they would be really grateful. Each comment carried an intimation or an innuendo – far from the innocent *Carry On* style of double entendre.

Only two or three minutes after I'd seen the SCD5 girl make a call, we were surrounded by four or five detectives. As we were hauled to our feet and handcuffed, one of the officers foolishly introduced himself, in full earshot of the customers, as being from the Paedophile Unit. So, if any of those diners, coffee sippers and staff at the café next to Barons Court Tube on that morning are reading this, I was not the paedophile!

Tony was charged with a grooming offence and went to prison for three years. When the case hit the papers, my partner's parents brought it to my attention because it was a scandal in their small town. To this day, they are blissfully unaware of my involvement in the case and how close they came to witnessing some of the evidence-gathering.

But while he spent 18 months inside, my own sentence proved to last a lot longer. Since then, I've never been able to erase from my mind the phone calls we had and the sick shit he spoke about. For months and years afterwards, if anyone came near my kids or spoke to them (whoever they were), I regarded them with deep suspicion. To this day, I think that everyone's intentions are dishonourable in some way. Thanks to the filth Tony spewed out, I even grew uncomfortable around my own kids' bathtime, because mention of the subject had been the catalyst for his obscene stories. I will never forgive him for tainting what should be an innocent experience. I try to forget, especially as I only dealt with it for a short while, but it's difficult.

These are feelings that I have resigned myself to having for the rest of my life. But I think it was worth it. I like to think I have saved at least one kid from a horrific experience, which no one, let alone a kid, should ever have to experience at the hands of a monster.

Back at the SO10 office, I got some begrudging compliments about the job, with some DSs even admitting that they would never have been able to do such an operation. I was pleased and, temporarily buoyed by the positivity, eagerly anticipated my next role.

21
SHOTGUNS IN CROYDON

'SO THAT'S ALL I HAVE TO DO?' I ASKED.

'Yep,' said Kevin, one of the SO10 DSs.

'OK,' I said. 'Fine.'

'Don't fuck it up, though,' he added for good measure.

Worried, I feigned a laugh.

Since being on the full-time unit, I hadn't seen too much of the 'traditional' side of undercover work, which was mainly buying drugs and guns. These were the jobs where the glamour and the action were. These were the jobs that got discussed in the pub or on the training courses. These were the jobs full of danger and excitement.

So, accidentally, I fell into this particular job. As is often the case, you would get assigned work by virtue of just passing through the SO10 office. Kevin grabbed me as I was wandering along the corridor and explained he was off on holiday and needed a stand-in on a job. We sat in the little SO10 meeting room.

'Right, I need you to go and buy a gun,' Kevin explained. 'It's in Croydon and it's all set up, a piece of piss.'

These were always the words you dreaded to hear. It was never that simple. 'OK,' I gulped.

I hate guns. Which is utterly ridiculous when you think I harboured ambitions to join the ranks of the Firearms Unit as a youngster. I'd only shot a gun on two occasions. One was a stag do in Budapest, with Hungarian ex-special forces 'instructors' encouraging the indiscriminate firing of a variety of weaponry down the 'range', a warehouse in a grotty industrial zone. This was in stark contrast to my other shooting experience, which was at the police firing range at Marylebone police station, watched over by a stern, officious firearms instructor, abiding by every health-and-safety rule under the sun.

Even on the undercover course, the teaching on firearms, which is a core business for SO10, accounted for only two hours and comprised a lot of storytelling with an opportunity to handle various types of gun. It is the policy that no UCO gets taught to shoot guns, because there's no need, and if you get taught to handle weapons like a cop, that's what you will do on the street, leading to the possibility of compromise.

'What am I buying?' I asked.

'A shotgun,' he said, calmly. 'Sawn-off, with shells.'

'Right.' I must have looked a bit nervous.

'Are you OK doing this? You happy with shotguns and how they work?' he said.

'Yeah, yeah, of course,' I lied, keen to get a 'real' job under my belt. In reality, I hadn't a clue and was quite anxious.

The next afternoon, I found myself at a briefing with the Met's Central Task Force, an elite detective squad that tackles serious gun and drug crime, housed in an anonymous office building and warehouse complex on the outskirts of London. I sat in the briefing room waiting for my instructions.

'Fuck me, not you, Christian!' boomed a deep Northern voice.

I turned and saw Dave, the gruff detective sergeant who had run my very first TP job. Now here he was running my latest UC job.

Happy to see a familiar face, I relaxed ever so slightly. But my frazzled mind buzzed and my stress levels rose as the room filled up. The Met, when it has decent enough intelligence, takes firearms crime very seriously. This was more than apparent as I sat in the briefing and what seemed like a battalion of armed cops trooped in, some in plain clothes, the outline of their 'covert' body armour visible under their North Face fleeces, Glocks attached to the belts of their faded blue 501s.

'Fuck,' I thought. 'This is all because I'm here to buy a gun. It's mental.' Once again, as I had done when I'd sat amongst hordes of cops for my first TP job, I felt butterflies in my stomach and my temples began to throb. I needed to concentrate, though. This was serious shit.

After the briefing, one of the Glocked-up firearms dudes approached. He had definitely got his swag on. 'All right, mate?' he said.

'Hello,' I replied, meekly.

'Right, the plan is we're gonna nick you and the target, so I need to know, have you ever been nicked at gunpoint?'

'Er, no.'

'OK. Well, there'll be a lot of guns about, all pointed in your direction. Some Tasers, too. Just do exactly as you're told. No one's gonna shoot you. All the guns are loaded and it'll look like they are pointed directly at you. Really, they'll be pointed at the target. We'll prone you out and PlastiCuff you, OK?'

'Er, OK.'

'If there's a gun knocking about, if you've bought one, we'll deal with it, OK?'

'All right,' I said.

I ditched my real identity, leaving my warrant card and personal effects with Dave. I tapped my back pocket, confirming that I had the wallet of my alter ego, Sulyenko, with me.

I had been allocated a permanent car, which, unfortunately, was a bright-blue Jaguar. Don't get me wrong, it was a nice motor. It had all the bells and whistles, including a TV. But I never quite felt comfortable driving it. It was the sort of motor a 60-year-old retired bank director drives, with his golf clubs in the back. I was, of course, loath to broach this subject at SO10, and indeed I was genuinely grateful that I'd even got a car. When I thought back to the multitude of occasions working on a crime squad or in CID when there were no motors available at all, or they broke down, I knew I was lucky.

This car was registered in one of my pseudonyms to a residential address that was a rented flat in south London, paid for by the firm. Personally, I thought it an utter waste of money. I visited the flat twice. I 'shared' the flat with another UC officer, and the idea was that we were to establish and maintain our aliases in that area, to bolster our credibility – legend-building. This mainly consisted of going to a local pub or bar and spending time 'getting our faces known'. The idea was that if a genuine criminal questioned us about our lives, we would have a real flat, a real local, a real gym, etc. It appeared that gyms and pubs were the necessary places to frequent to acquire new chums of a dubious nature.

As far as legend-building was concerned, I only conducted this a few times. First, I gave it little credence, and thought that needlessly drinking in a pub I didn't really want to be in wouldn't be beneficial. Second, I had far more important things to do out of work, particularly with the concerns about our unborn baby.

I jumped into the Jag and fired her up. The meeting was to take place in a Sainsbury's car park in Thornton Heath. I was on my way to meet Faisal, who had already arranged to sell the gun to Kevin for £2,500. I had drawn the cash out at the Yard, and it was now tucked into the spare wheel in the Jag's boot.

I had to get to the car park about 20 minutes early so that the surveillance team that would be following me and Faisal could 'plot up' and begin their observations. In the event, I got there about half an hour early and, as the barrier raised to let me in, I decided to park a few yards from the store entrance.

I was able to contact my cover officer for the job, Max, and let him know I was in place. Max was with the DI running the entire show, and anything I needed to communicate would go through Max.

My nerves were frayed. As I waited, my throat got dry and constricted, and I began to go through loads of horrific scenarios. What if he made me drive into some dead end? What if the surveillance team and the firearms bods lost me? What if, what if, what if? I was, as usual, absolutely bricking it. Still, something pushed me to carry on regardless.

About five minutes before the arranged time, I called Faisal and told him I had just arrived. He simply said, 'Wait there,' and put the phone down.

Wiggling my legs, as if I needed a wee, and furiously biting my fingernails, I had to wait no more than two or three minutes. A young lad pitched up, around 20 years old. He looked at me and nodded, before eyeing up the car suspiciously. 'Shit,' I thought. 'He's obviously been here a while. Did he see me come in? Did he see any of the surveillance team?'

He got in.

'All right, bruv?' I said, reverting to street-scum TPO mode, despite the Jag.

'You're Kevin's mate, yeah?' he said.

'Yep,' I said. 'So, what about this bit of business?'

'It ain't here, fam,' he said. 'Just drive. I'll tell you where.'

Now definitely a bit worried, I drove towards the car park exit.

Shit. Shit. Shit. You needed a fucking ticket to get out if you'd been here for more than half an hour. Bollocks, I thought. Still, I nonchalantly drove up to the barrier and waited for it to open. When it didn't, I wound the window down and indignantly stabbed at the intercom.

'Hallo,' shouted the attendant through the tinny, inadequate speaker.

'Hello, boss,' I called. 'I can't get out.'

'Yeah, you need a ticket, my friend,' replied the almost indecipherable African voice over the intercom.

'What for? I only got here ten minutes ago.'

'No, no, no, no,' said the voice. 'You got here 37 minutes ago. I've been watching you on camera.'

Fuck. I glanced at Faisal. He was looking very uncomfortable.

'What the fuck!' I screamed. 'That's bollocks, mate. Let me out this fucking car park now.'

I regretted the outburst, but luckily the car park dude presumably couldn't be bothered to argue and the barrier was raised without further discussion.

'Prick!' I shouted as I drove away.

Faisal shifted in the passenger seat. I glanced in my rear-view mirror as we drove, trying to identify some of the surveillance vehicles, but I couldn't. I just had to hope that they were behind me.

Faisal directed me, monosyllabically, through seemingly endless south London back streets. Eventually, we turned into a dead-end street and Faisal directed me to a small car park in front of a block of flats. This was the very scenario that I had been worrying about earlier. Still, no time for fucking about. I couldn't see anyone in my rear-view mirror and hadn't done so for a while. Where the fuck was the surveillance team? I didn't even know what road I was on. Shit.

Faisal told me to wait and got out of the car, it seemed to make a phone call. I speed-dialled Max's number and, leaving the line open, dropped the phone into my lap, knowing that Max would be totally au fait with what was going on and would listen.

Faisal got back in the car, and I nervously began to make small talk before pointing to the tower block and saying, 'Oh, Florence Nightingale House? I'm sure my nan used to live here,' in a desperate attempt to get Max to hear my location on the open phone line.

'Hmm,' answered Faisal, still slightly edgy. He looked at me as if I was from another planet, and I think he was about to say something when a young boy of no more than eight rode up on a bike to the passenger window and handed Faisal a rolled-up JD Sports bag.

The lad quickly pedalled away as Faisal dumped the bag in my lap. Hoping that this would be over soon, I unravelled the bag in the foot well and opened it up. Inside was an old and slightly rusty sawn-off single-barrelled shotgun. In addition, I could see three or four cartridges rolling around.

'Fuck me,' I said. 'It's a fucking antique. Does it work?'

'Yeah, course it does,' Faisal replied.

I gingerly handled the stock and searched for the little catch I wanted to open it up, mainly to make sure it wasn't loaded but also to check it wasn't blocked or filthy and therefore useless. I sound like I knew what I was doing, but I hadn't the faintest idea, in all seriousness. All I remembered from the UC course was the edict that if there is a little switch on a gun with cross-hatchings on it, then it is designed to be pushed, pulled, lifted or turned, and that's often to do something useful. So, lo and behold, I found a little switch, pushed it to one side and cracked open the gun. Phew, empty.

I glanced at Faisal and said, hopefully with the requisite amount of authority, 'Yeah, looks fine. Let me bell Kevin.'

At that moment, a load of shaven-headed cops in Timberlands and Berghaus jackets came steaming in. They were also wearing thigh holsters, body armour, ballistic helmets and goggles, and I did fleetingly think, 'Why didn't you just wear a uniform?'

An unmarked Mercedes Veto van screeched sideways in front of us and these guys poured out, guns pointed, flashlights lit.

'Armed police, armed police! Show me your hands. Now!' came the screamed commands. Three or four cops at the front of my car had machine guns and pistols pointed at me. Another guy stood by with a Taser.

'Armed police! Do NOT fucking move!' one of them shouted.

'OK, OK,' the little posh voice in my head noted. 'I'm not moving, I'm not moving!'

I raised my hands, saying, 'Shit,' as my door was yanked open and I was hauled out onto the roadway, a Glock pointed at me for maximum theatrical effect. Before I had time to think, I was face down and handcuffed on the ground. 'Please don't smash the car up,' I thought. Had it been a baddie's car, they would have battered the crap out of it for 'distraction reasons', but they were all aware that this one belonged to SO10.

'Gun!' shouted one of the armed cops, as they found the sawn-off in the foot well. I could see directly underneath the car; on the other side, Faisal was also pinned to the ground and handcuffed.

It was a strange moment when we looked at each other, at ground level, from either side of my car, both our faces squashed against the rough asphalt. We shared a long glance before he turned his head away. His face was expressionless.

I could see lots of Timberlands, Merrell trainers and Hi-Tec Magnums milling around on Faisal's side of the car. I heard someone say, 'Right, whose is the car?'

I saw Faisal twist his head round to face me, staring at me intently, both of us still prone on the ground. He shouted out the answer to that question himself. 'It's OK, it's the officer's car.' He grinned malevolently at me. 'Yeah, it's the officer's car,' he repeated a little more quietly, and turned his head away from me again.

He probably suspected when he met me but had been willing to take the risk. I often think to myself, if he knew, he could have walked off with the boy, put the shells in the gun, shot me and no one could have stopped him.

After his wry comment, I was convinced I couldn't use that car again. I didn't fancy driving around in it given that anyone who had seen me get arrested could have memorised the number plate. In south London, I was doing things with the Source Development Unit, I was doing things with the Eastern European UC officers. It was not beyond the realms of possibility that someone with links to a Turkish gun-smuggling gang could have spotted me and said, 'That's the guy that put whatshisname away, let's kill him.'

I said as much to the guy in charge of the cars. 'I think this car might be compromised,' I told him. 'Any chance I can get another one?'

He said, 'Nah, we don't have any others available.'

I had to give them my audio recording of the whole episode. It is quite stressful being dragged out of a car at gunpoint at the best of times, but everyone seemed to think you were superhuman. The attitude was that it was your job and you could take it. We managed to get a gun off the street, so it was a good result.

Shortly afterwards, I got a phone call from a DS at the full-time unit.

'Can you come to Scotland Yard straight away?' he asked. 'The DI wants to see you urgently.'

Could it be praise for a job well done?

22

THE END OF AN ERA

BONG!

The door alarm of the shop chimed. A customer. I knew the cameras and microphones had gone live as soon as the door had opened and that the operational team, housed in a nondescript flat 15 miles away, would be monitoring what went on.

'Hello, mate,' I said to the gaunt, pasty-faced lad.

'Awright, bruv. You buyin' passports?'

'Yes, mate, whatever you got,' I answered wearily, knowing what was coming.

The lad looked around furtively.

'Shut the door, mate,' I said across the shoulder-level counter. He turned, closed the shop door and slid a purple passport across the counter.

I opened it to examine it. It was genuine. The photo inside, obviously taken some time ago, I recognised immediately, the baby face not yet strained or wearied by the complexities of young life in inner-city London.

'It's yours,' I said to the lad.

'Yeah, I know, bruv. Man say you're buying, innit?'

'This is fucking ridiculous,' I thought. 'Hundreds of

thousands of quid of taxpayers' money, the latest technology, full-time UC officers, and here we are buying people's own passports off them. Fuck me.'

I pulled out a wad of cash and handed the youngster 150 quid. No flicker of thanks or a smile passed over his face as he took it and stuffed it into the pocket of his low-slung Nike track pants.

People came in selling all sorts of boot-sale shit. I felt sorry for every single one of them. Even the so-called 'main target', a career burglar, was going out nicking stuff just for us. If we hadn't been there, he wouldn't have nicked stuff. Simple. This was not what I had joined the Old Bill for, and it certainly wasn't what I expected to be doing on an elite unit.

Other colleagues were working guns and drugs jobs, but even so I wasn't jealous. I had far too much on my plate to be bothered about that. I was nothing more than a glorified shop monkey, doing a job that I didn't agree with and which I was unequivocally unwedded to.

This was my first 'long-term' job. Along with Terry, the 'main' UC on the job, I was expected to be here every day, work the shop, then go out – you've guessed it – drinking in the local pub until all hours, staying the night in a locally rented flat. Terry, a vastly superior UC than I could ever wish to be, was a family man. He had just finished a two-year-long job up north and hardly ever saw his family. No way could I ever commit to that at the moment. I had gone to training school 16 years ago with Terry, so I knew him anyway and got on well with him. I made it clear to him that my other half was pregnant and that it was a difficult time. I told him, and indeed the DI running the operation, that I couldn't commit to the long-drawn-out days and nights that I should have done. I made that utterly crystal. Terry was fine about it. I have no idea whether the DI was or not.

Simply put, however, I shouldn't have been doing this sort of job, which required a certain level of commitment.

First off, I was told to hang around a pub. Surprise, eh? I managed to pop in a few times over the course of four weeks or so. It was dire, again, just like in the job I had mysteriously been shoehorned out of in Romford at The Tramshed. I found it difficult, if not impossible, to get to the pub in the evenings, when it was apparently busy. In any case, my intention, as with the Tramshed job, was to spend a few weeks hanging around during the daytime, get to know the staff and punters, and eventually start going there in the evenings.

To help me out in spending time at this den of iniquity, in which the most criminal thing I ever saw was the landlord's dress sense, I bought membership at the local gym. In addition, I bought gym kit and other accoutrements. Naturally, I paid for all this out of my covert funds. The receipts got chucked onto the pile with the rest. I didn't know what I was buying with what card or on what account. I had completely lost track of it all. I didn't know who I was meant to be in this new pub, so, dangerously, I carried two different sets of ID with me.

In any case, I joined the gym, trying to live up to the SO10 ideal of frequenting gyms and pubs. I probably went twice. Another waste of money. I joined a yoga gym in West London too, to assist with my legend for the operation with the East European operatives. Again, I went there twice, probably.

I simply didn't want to be at work. I was far too worried about the baby and Grace. It ate at my mind constantly. I carried my personal mobile phone with me all the time, which was generally frowned upon. It contained hundreds of numbers of cops and nicks as well as photos of me and colleagues in police stations, in police cars, all that sort of stuff. Had it been found by a villain (not that there was ever any chance of consorting with any, I thought), I would have been knackered.

After a few weeks of little intelligence use, I was told that I now had to concentrate on the main part of the operation and work with Terry in the cash-converters-style store in Cricklewood. Ostensibly a gold merchant-cum-pawnbroker, the shop bought absolutely anything.

The idea, of course, was to tempt the local burglars and robbers to bring their ill-gotten gains to the shop. Which was all well and good; however, while there was a lot of criminal property coming in, it soon became obvious that our promise to 'ask no questions' had backfired somewhat, with all and sundry, particularly crackheads and heroin users, bringing in their passports, bank cards, cheque books, NI cards and driving licences to sell, and for a fair amount of cash too. We were giving 150 quid for a passport – not a bad return for a down-on-his-luck crackhead who is unlikely to be booking a holiday to the Costa del Sol any time soon.

I think the only proper criminal I met in there was a local guy who had committed burglaries in the past. I remember pulling up outside the shop in a white van, the Jaguar having been reissued to someone else.

'Hello, mate,' he said. 'You Terry's pal, yeah?'

'Yeah,' I answered cautiously.

'Oh, OK. Just worried, that's all,' he said.

'Oh, why?'

'Your van looks like one of them ones the Old Bill use to do surveillance, that's all. Dead fucking giveaway if you ask me – ladder rack on the roof and no ladders.'

'Oh, yeah,' I said. 'Me mate's got the ladders.' (Worried

I might be getting pinged for a cop in a surveillance van, I drove round the corner later and bought some aluminium ladders for the van.)

'Oh, OK,' he replied happily. 'Tell Terry I was about, OK?'

'OK,' I replied, puzzled.

I got the impression that this guy was dealing only with Terry. I think he had passed on a few nicked computers or something. I had the feeling he wasn't a professional, just a guy with a drug habit. To be honest, I reckon if the shop hadn't been there, he wouldn't have nicked anything to sell to us.

I was really quite uncomfortable with this but made no mention of it. I was particularly non-proactive at the shop. I liked the regular hours. I would open the shop, chat with Terry all day, close up at the end of business and drive home. That suited me. I had little to offer in the way of police work. I would constantly be on the phone to home or nipping off for hospital appointments and suchlike.

Yet this was the job the DI had been in such a hurry to see me about after the shotgun job. When I'd got that call, I had no idea what was up. I knew it wouldn't really be anything positive. That's not their style. But then I thought it might have been because of my expenses. I'd been neglecting them badly, and sooner or later I expected SO10 to come down on me. I had all this other shit going on. Everything was starting to build up.

In many ways, I felt relieved. 'Thank fuck for that,' I thought. 'They've realised I haven't been doing my expenses. I'll get a bollocking and maybe some help with doing them. Maybe they'll even say I can have a couple of weeks off.' Far from it. Instead, it was the start of things going seriously downhill.

The DI had wanted to see me at 3 p.m. I texted the DS at 2.50 p.m. to say I was stuck in a bit of traffic and I'd be there as quick as I could. I turned up in the office at 3.10 p.m. and went in to see the DI.

'Really sorry I'm late. I texted to say I was stuck in traffic.'

'That's not fucking good enough,' the DI said.

'What?' I said. 'Are you joking?' I seriously thought he might be, because that's the type of stupid thing that they do.

'I was sorting out my evidence for the gun job.'

'I don't give a fuck,' he snarled. 'Don't ever turn up late for a meeting with me.'

I thought, 'OK, you're trying to be all inspector-ish, maybe there's someone in the room you're trying to impress.'

I said again, 'You are joking, aren't you? I'm really sorry.'

'No, I'm not fucking joking.'

'If I've offended you, I am really sorry.'

'Right, well, it doesn't matter. We have another job for you.'

And so he handed me the details for the cash-converter job. In hindsight, it was the worst sort of operation I could have been on. I started falling to bits almost immediately. My transition from the SDU to the full-time unit hadn't been handled very well at all. Everyone in the SDU knew I was having personal issues. In fact, my DS would regularly comment that I had had a year of being the golden boy and suddenly I was demotivated.

In many ways, my case shows up failings in the system. I was surprised that going full-time didn't require a selection procedure or further psychological assessment. They should have known at SO10 – it was all part of the same covert world as the SDU – either by someone saying it officially or by someone mentioning it casually, that I was having a traumatic time. I wish that someone had said, 'You are not in a suitable position to come up here.' I wouldn't be writing this now if they had.

I thought that if I got on the full-time unit, it would take my mind off my problems. I hoped it would be a fairly autonomous working environment and I could do what I wanted. That turned out not to be the case.

One day, in the store, I got a call from Grace, in tears and very upset. 'I'm bleeding,' she said, 'and it won't stop.'

Fuck. I called out to Terry that I was going. He replied, 'Yeah, that's fine, mate.'

As I drove, seatbelt off and way over the speed limit, to the hospital, I realised that I really couldn't be arsed with this job any more. After doing only a few UC jobs, it hit me that I had way more important shit to think about and that I really couldn't devote the time I'd been able to back in the day. But for now I just needed to get to the hospital.

Breathless, sweating and shaking with nerves, I finally found Grace. She was fine, thank God.

Something inside me had clicked. It was time to get a new job, I thought, something interesting but utterly stress free. I needed out of the police. I'd had enough. I had something in mind.

I think this swift exit from the shop was the last straw for the DI running the job. The next day, I drove, as usual, to our regular weekly meeting of full-time UC officers and SO10 DSs. The meeting took place in a nondescript building where you went once a week for a briefing or a bollocking.

Each of us gave a brief summary of what we had been up to and what was happening the next week. The DSs gave a rundown on what was happening in the organisation and any pertinent news, and that was generally it.

As we all rose to leave, one of the DSs, Kevin, called out, 'Christian, wait here a sec. We need a chat.'

The tone was ominous. I knew it. I fucking knew it. 'About bloody time,' I thought, expecting a stern telling off about my lack of expenses submissions, a boot up the arse and to be given a deadline to have them in by. I was almost pleased. At last, I would get this off my chest and someone in authority would see that I needed some sort of help, or a big bollocking to get me back on track.

I was nervous, because it meant admitting I had fucked up, that I had neglected an essential aspect of paperwork and that I couldn't be responsible enough to comply with an archaic system I didn't actually understand.

I sat down with Kevin and Max. They had my 'duty state', a handwritten record of the hours I had worked, for last week in front of them. I could also see an expenses form. 'OK,' began Kevin. 'There's been some questions asked about your commitment to the job. Apparently, you haven't been putting the hours in.'

I was aghast. I knew that my work ethic had dwindled considerably, and that my commitment, interest and enthusiasm had petered out to almost nothing, but somehow to hear it said out loud was really shockingly upsetting.

Kevin explained that the DI from the Cricklewood job had questioned the hours I had put into the job and the hours on my duty state. Fuck me, that was outrageous. The fiddling of duty states is a very common practice on squads where they are still used. I had never claimed any more hours than I was entitled to, and I told Kevin as much.

Max thrust an expenses form at me. 'You seem to be buying a lot of cappuccinos and lattes,' he said.

'Yeah, I drink a lot of coffee,' I said.

'But you're buying three or four coffees a day,' he said.

'And? I drink a lot of coffee.' My love of Starbucks was generally known.

'And buying it in Waltham Abbey?' he asked. 'What's that got to do with the job you're doing in Cricklewood?'

I said that as soon as I left home, driving a UC car registered in a pseudonym, I was that person. I said that maybe I had misunderstood the general consensus that my expenses, while undercover, would be paid for.

'No. Don't be ridiculous. The DI is refusing to sanction these coffees,' said Max.

'OK, I'll resubmit the form then,' I said, red-faced.

'Look,' said Kevin, 'I know you've got personal problems, and they are none of my business, but do you really think that you should be doing this type of work at the moment?'

'Probably not,' I replied, tearfully.

'Well, the fact of the matter is, I think you want the lifestyle but don't want to do the work.'

It was at that moment that the magic SO10 tractor beam released me and I hit reality with a thump. I was cross and upset. I was a fucking good copper, and now I was reduced to tears explaining buying cappuccinos in front of people from a department that had sanctioned much worse. After my first job in Park Lane, no words had been said about other officers coming and partaking of the meal and drinks after the baddie had left! No one questioned the firm paying for nights out on the lash! No one questioned me paying for a sumptuous meal for other officers on my credit card – in fact I was almost ordered to do it! And yet here I was justifying some coffee. And being accused of fiddling my hours was just the worst.

In my head I repeated what Kevin had just said: 'You want the lifestyle but don't want to do the work.'

Never, ever had I been accused of being workshy. I was horrified.

'The lifestyle?' I replied, choking back tears. 'What? Of not knowing who I am? Not knowing who I'm supposed to be that day? Remembering what number plates I've got on the car? Buying passports off crackheads? What, that lifestyle? No, I never wanted that lifestyle.'

'Well,' said Max, 'we need to decide what action to take and what to do.'

'Do you know what?' I said. 'I was gonna tell you next week, but I'm resigning anyway. I've got a new job.'

'Well, there's nothing more to say,' said Max with finality, slamming shut the folder in front of him.

EPILOGUE

TO GET INTO THIS WORLD WAS HARD. FOR ME, IT MEANT pretending to be someone else, a person who I did not like and who I would not tolerate. I had to be 'undercover' to get into the undercover world. To be part of that world, you had to be subservient and ingratiating, and do a lot of kowtowing and sucking up. This meant joining in the banter. It meant being a nasty fucker to non-UCs and wannabe TPs.

So, you may ask, why the fuck would I want to be part of that? The best reason, and here comes the amateur psychology, was because I had always doubted myself. I think the phrase 'low self-esteem' is always a handy excuse. I certainly wasn't a hard man. I wasn't a rufty-tufty type – more of a lover than a fighter. But I deeply wanted to prove myself in this very male, very difficult and hard-to-break world. I really wanted a part of it – the kudos and the status. These guys, for all their faults, were the most knowledgeable and experienced guys in the covert world. I, rather mistakenly, thought that if I could get in there I would have made it. I would be satisfied. I wouldn't have to prove myself to myself. I was constantly yearning for more, something challenging and out of my comfort zone. Most of these blokes came across as gangster-esque. On the one hand, I derided them for it. On the other hand, I wanted to be them. It was an odd confluence of admiration and dislike.

Since leaving, it has been hard coming to terms with a lot of things. Just before I left officially, my beautiful baby boy was born. He is my opportunity almost to live my life again, as if I have another chance.

I haven't kept in touch with too many people. I hear a lot of gossip on the grapevine. Some think I was sacked. Some think I am now a homeless junkie. Others apparently think I am still working undercover and my resignation was all part of the plan. Ridiculous stories like this only make me more glad of my decision to leave the police.

After my meeting with Max and Kevin, I only had one more chat, about paperwork. After that, I barely spoke to anyone from the Met Police again. I was vetted to the highest level, so I was expecting an interview with the vetting department, but it never transpired. With someone of my status, you're supposed to have an interview with a senior line manager about why you're leaving. The Met did nothing like that with me. It was as though they were happy to wash their hands of me.

I saw the psychologist – a meeting that had been arranged before I resigned after I'd referred myself. I was looking forward to a final debrief with him. He usually asked the question, 'Have you had any suicidal thoughts?' I intended to come clean and tell him everything, blurt it all out and get it off my chest. I wanted to tell him about the day when I had intended to chuck myself off a ferry, tell him about my succession of fuck-ups. He never asked the question. The only time I wanted him to, he never asked! When I told him I was leaving, he said, 'There's no point in doing any of this then,' before adding, somewhat reluctantly, it seemed, 'But we still have a duty of care.' Nothing further came of that.

I gathered all my property up and dumped it on a desk. I had dozens of phones, a sat nav and other bits I had bought with my covert cards. I returned it all. I thought they'd log it, but it was like a free-for-all. Everyone was picking up the equipment and phones, saying, 'Ooh, this is a nice one,' and pocketing it.

On my last day in the job, I sat down in the SDU office to face my nemesis: the dreaded expenses forms. I filled out months and months' worth of expenses claims and put the forms, along with the receipts, my resignation letter, my birth certificate and other bits and bobs in big brown envelopes addressed to the relevant department. Funnily enough, they received my resignation letter but mysteriously not my expenses claims.

After that, I left the building, turned my back on the police and went home.

My really good friend Bernard, who all those years ago had introduced me to the intriguing secret world of test purchase work and was now a detective chief inspector, phoned me not long after I resigned and said, 'What are you doing? Has anyone spoken to you about this?' When I explained the situation, he told me, 'That's outrageous.'

He contacted the detective chief superintendent in charge of covert ops. Bernard said, 'Has someone spoken with Christian Plowman? He's resigning. He's one of the best police officers I've ever worked with. Someone needs to get hold of him and speak to him. He's not the type of person we should be allowing to leave.'

This DCS – who a few weeks before had presented me with a commendation for the Manchester gun job – said, 'Christian who?'